Breathing Space

A 52-Week Meditation Journey for Centered, Soulful, and Successful Living

Kevin Kitrell Ross
Eric Ovid Donaldson

Books may be purchased in quantity and/or special sales by contacting the publisher.

Mynd Matters Publishing
715 Peachtree Street NE
Suites 100 & 200
Atlanta, GA 30308
www.myndmatterspublishing.com

Paperback ISBN: 978-1-953307-37-8
Hardcover ISBN: 978-1-953307-38-5

FIRST EDITION

To a breathless world weary with the fatigue of a double pandemic. May these pages offer you a safe space to exhale, rebuild, and repossess your breath and the promise it is for humanity's future.

Contents

PART V

PART VI

PART VII

PART VIII

PART IX

PART X

PART XI

PART XII

Introduction

Welcome to the *Breathing Space* meditation journey! We call it *Breathing Space*, because we realize that in our work-obsessed, dog-eat-dog, nonstop culture, most people are unconsciously suffering due to a deficit of stillness, a malnourished inner spirit, and a body void of sufficient oxygen. Plainly, we are often so overworked, over stressed, and overwhelmed that we are often simply out of breath. So, we have created this guide to help you repossess your breath and maintain conscious possession of your breath from all the ways it gets taken by stress, drama, trauma, busyness, and even blessings.

This 52-week experience was designed to support you with establishing or supplementing your own daily practice that deepens your connection to Spirit and compels you to design and live a centered, soulful, and successful life. With *Breathing Space*, you have an inspired guide to support you with creating daily sacred space for inner stillness, deep breathing, weekly inspirational writing, and ample reflection space. This space is to process the insights, revelations, and successes that result from using this journal. We take the legwork out of finding a positive thought for you to center upon in meditation. This process has it all. All you need is a little time, a quiet spot, an ink pen, and an open mind!

Simply, the *Breathing Space* meditation journey is designed to slow down the pace of the busy surface mind so you can learn to savor and luxuriate in the intricate beauty of your emerging life. While similar inspirational guides provide you with a daily meditative thought, to get the most out of such a reading, we realize that it is helpful to provide "space" to center, contemplate, and commune with the indwelling Spirit.

This process will allow you to take a deep dive into the mystical aspect of your soul by providing you with a word to think about, a declaration to speak about, a meditative thought to sit with, and a reflection question to contemplate.

There are also quotes throughout the reading, from some of our most inspired thought leaders, Way Showers, avatars and ancient scripture. This too is intended to whet your appetite for deeper study. We would hope that as these quotes speak to you, that you might research the author(s) and delve into their published works more fully to incorporate their wisdom into your spiritual development curriculum. Finally, we have also included some of our favorite images from our personal archives and from renowned Miami artist and photographer, Rhonda Gutierrez, so that during your Breathing Space journey, you may simply "gaze" upon them and allow them to transport you into the spaces of serenity, bliss, and peace that they represent. And since people all over the world will be walking through this process as well, you have access to a community of like-minded friends you can connect with to share insights or to take the entire 52-week journey alongside. Please visit www.kevinrossinspires.com/breathingspace to join our online community. When you get there, post a picture of you with your book, and show us your favorite space for experiencing Breathing Space.

Your Breathing Space Journey is designed to serve you, and you can use this guide for 52 weeks, beginning at any point of a given year that you choose. In the same way you might enter a hiking trail, there is really no prescribed start point or end point. What we have done is made it a 52-week alphabetical journey. That is, each of the Weekly Topics are in order from A to Z. Feel free to take the journey in sequence or move ahead to a topic that jumps out at you. By the way, this guide is not another run of the mill "standard" guide with the usual topics. It is a mixed bag of important themes from attitude to xenophobia. So strap in and get ready for an inward journey of a lifetime!

Ready to get started?

Here's how to get the most from your *Breathing Space* meditation journey. Take a moment to walk through these steps as they will serve as gentle guides to support you with easing into your journey and taking full ownership of your practice.

In the same way most people carve out at least thirty minutes per day to work out their physical bodies, *Breathing Space* provides quadruple the value in half the time. By committing to a minimum of fifteen focused minutes a day to this mindfulness practice, we are confident you will grow more centered, soulful, and successful and as you appreciate the process you may choose to lengthen the time you dedicate to it daily.

Follow these steps to jumpstart your journey:

1. Commit to taking the Breathing Space 52-Week Challenge. Once you start the journey, see it all the way through! Even if you miss a day, pick up where you leave off.

2. Establish a consistent time of day when you will use this guide.

3. Set aside at least fifteen minutes per day to complete your daily practice.

4. Create a sacred space in which you will engage in your practice. ***Sacred space*** is what you make of it. However, what's most important is that it's yours. We suggest you have a quiet space that will allow you to be undistracted for at least fifteen to twenty minutes of your practice. We also suggest you consider bringing any elements into the space

that add to your inner experience of reverence, calm, and centeredness. Some may choose to light a candle, play soft music, burn incense, use a diffuser, sit in a favorite chair, or open a nearby window to hear the ocean or sounds of nature. Regardless of your choice, the intention in creating a sacred space is to enlarge your sense of being centered and connected. The environment should be attractive to you and give you a sense of being supported and it should inspire you to return again and again.

5. Select your favorite type of writing instrument. With this suggestion, we want you to have all parts of this 52-week long practice to include components that entice you to take the entire journey. We know what it's like to write using a favorite pen. You begin to associate the practice with something you love—your favorite space, your favorite seat, and your favorite writing instrument.

6. Take the journey with at least one other person—if not several people. We learn and grow more when we share the journey with individuals who are willing to go with us, but also hold us accountable to our commitment.

7. Trust the process. As you begin to utilize the various components of the Breathing Space Meditation Journey, you will establish a rhythm, a pattern, and a pace that are uniquely your own. Go with that. Do not feel pressured to complete a day's entry in the same day you start it. You determine the length of a day. Complete the entry when you have had an insight you are ready to jot down. We suggest you move through your weekly process with this three-fold pattern in mind:

Inhale – Hold—Exhale

Inhale: Take in the reading. Ingest it. Enjoy it. Completely consume it.

Hold: Reflect upon it. Sit with it. Dissect it. Contemplate it. Luxuriate in it.

Exhale: Jot down your insights, revelations, and celebrations.

Repeat this process for the six Daily Question prompts. Each prompt will support you with reflecting on the meditative thought by asking you to look at how does the reading:

Center You
Call You
Challenge You
Clarify You
Comfort You
Change You

We are confident that by using this process you will dissolve your stress, open your heart, expand your consciousness and heighten your skies. We look forward to hearing from you about your journey. Meanwhile, remember to breathe!

Mystically yours,
Rev. Kev
Kevin Kitrell Ross

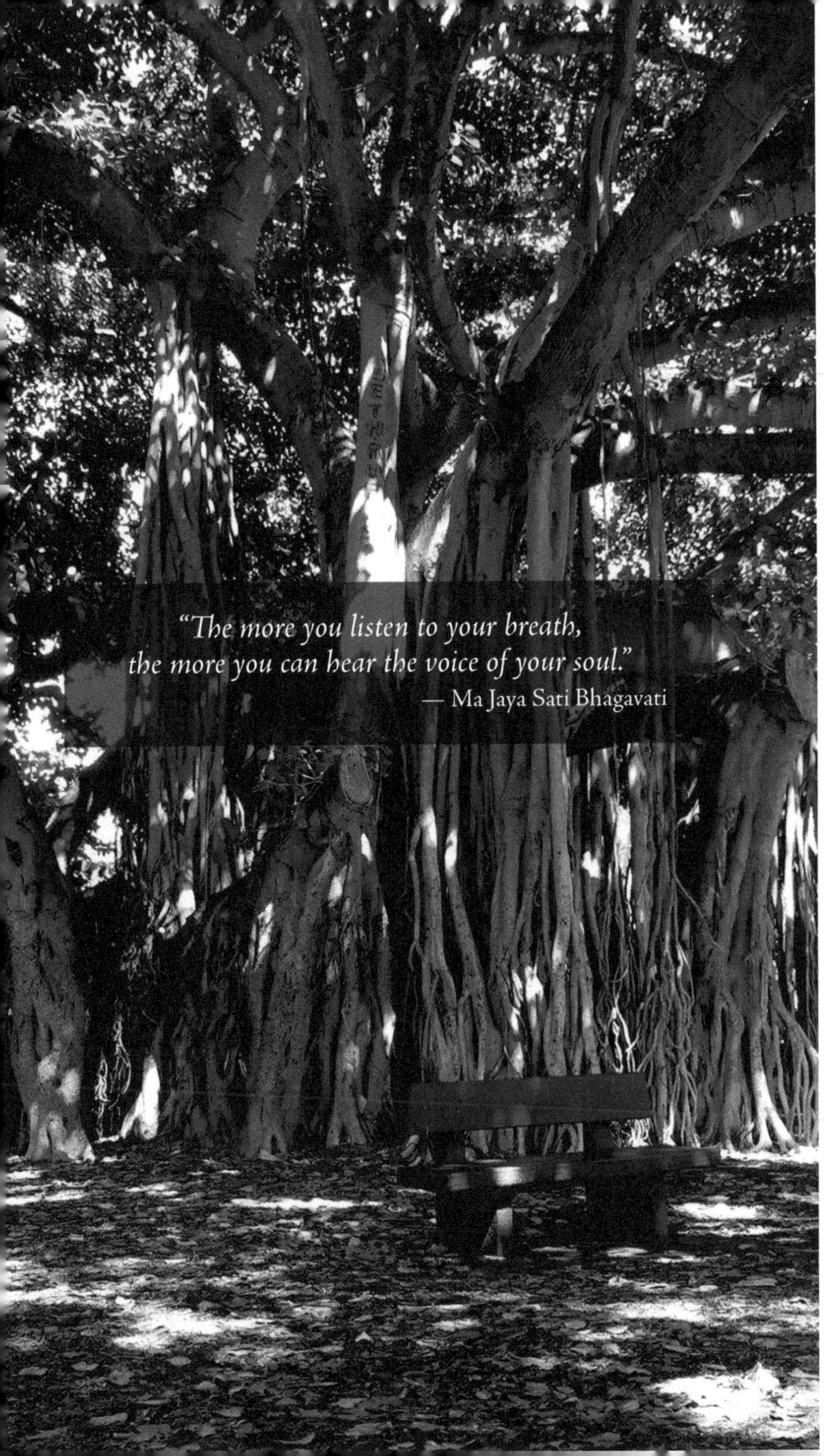
"The more you listen to your breath,
the more you can hear the voice of your soul."
— Ma Jaya Sati Bhagavati

3 AM Friend

I AM blessed by the treasure of my most cherished friendships.

"And let there be no purpose in friendship save the deepening of the spirit."

— Khalil Kibran

They are your sweet relief. The warm voice of comfort. The strong shoulder to lean on. The lifter of your head. The guilty laughter at things remembered. The wise and trusted voice of correction. The extra set of hands in handling the not-so-glamorous tasks in life. The first to arrive and the last to leave on the big day. The name at the top of your emergency call list.

They are the keeper of your secrets. The conspirator in your hair-brained schemes. The fact checker of your memories. The celebrant who makes the loudest splash. They are the exhale amidst the tension and your sigh of relief when you are stranded at midnight on the roadside.

Visit often, with a bow of gratitude, that special place in your heart set aside for your 3 AM Friend and gift yourself with gladness. Count it a privilege to have found just one in a lifetime. They are more rare than the sighting of a shooting star, a solar eclipse, or any earthly phenomenon. For indeed, they are evidence of a cosmic fact. Just as a single star has its galaxies, and the sun its planets, so too have we been given our friends.

3 AM Friend

REFLECTION QUESTION

How often are you filled with gratitude for your 3 AM friend(s) and what expressions of appreciation have you shown them lately?

WEEK 1

3 AM Friend

I AM blessed by the treasure of my most cherished friendships.

Day 2

CENTER

How does this week's reading CENTER me and bring calm, balance, and breathing space to my worldview?

Day 3

CALL

How does this week's reading CALL to me? How am I being awakened with a greater sense of purpose and spirituality? How am I inspired to be a force for good in the world?

Day 4

CHALLENGE

How does this week's reading CHALLENGE me to grow? What am I now ready to adjust, release, forgive, and accept as a result of this week's reading?

WEEK 1

Day 5 **CLARITY**

What new CLARITY have I gained as a result of this week's reading? What better understanding do I now possess?

Day 6 **COMFORT**

What brings me COMFORT about this week's reading? How am I more at ease or consoled by this week's reading?

Day 7 **CHANGE**

How am I CHANGED by this week's reading? What insights, transforming thoughts, inner realizations, overcomings and breakthroughs am I now experiencing?

Amends

I humbly and promptly clean up what I mess up and speed the way to healing.

"God grant me the serenity to accept the person I cannot change, to change the person that I can, and the wisdom to know that the person is me."

— Unknown

Face it. Despite our best intentions, we all mess up. We all make mistakes. We all get it wrong from time to time. We all hurt someone's feelings, and at times, we even sabotage ourselves. This is a part of our human journey. While we all miss the mark, how we respond can make the difference in our growth. The tendency to defend ourselves, double down on our positions or avoid the consequences of our actions, only prolongs the rift created by the offense.

In the final analysis, our greatest assets in the Earth School are our relationships. Among the ways we can benefit by our mistakes, is by choosing to "take credit" for the ways in which we have fallen short—without all the drama. Own the breakdown in communication. Own the error in judgement. Own the disloyalty. Own the betrayal. Simply, own it. "Taking credit" is accepting responsibility for the ways in which we fallen short or created pain for someone else—either intentionally or unintentionally.

A clear indication that you have taken credit is through actions to heal the relationship by humbly apologizing, accepting responsibility, and making amends. When we have truly made amends, we have learned and carried out the action that would bring healing to the party we offended. We live another day; not free from mistakes, but better equipped to handle them.

REFLECTION QUESTION

Where and with whom do you need to clean it up and take credit for the ways in which you have fallen short?

WEEK 2

I humbly and promptly clean up what I mess up and speed the way to healing.

Day 2 **CENTER**

How does this week's reading CENTER me and bring calm, balance, and breathing space to my worldview?

Day 3 **CALL**

How does this week's reading CALL to me? How am I being awakened with a greater sense of purpose and spirituality? How am I inspired to be a force for good in the world?

Day 4 **CHALLENGE**

How does this week's reading CHALLENGE me to grow? What am I now ready to adjust, release, forgive, and accept as a result of this week's reading?

WEEK

2

Day 5 **CLARITY**

What new CLARITY have I gained as a result of this week's reading? What better understanding do I now possess?

Day 6 **COMFORT**

What brings me COMFORT about this week's reading? How am I more at ease or consoled by this week's reading?

Day 7 **CHANGE**

How am I CHANGED by this week's reading? What insights, transforming thoughts, inner realizations, overcomings and breakthroughs am I now experiencing?

Anew!

My new year is my new norm that catapults my unprecedented future!

"In the beginning…God."
— Genesis 1:1

Bring them in with explosive celebration! Ring them in with glasses that cling. Dance them in with jubilant and colorful expression. March them in with cadence and numbers that sing. Pray them in with sacred reverence. Shout them on bended knee. Write them in with cautious reflection. Fill them in with bold reverie.

Your new year is at last upon you, charging you with duty and task. And yesteryear is expunged from among you, holding no record of the past. So take it on with reckless abandon. Stamp on it the markings of your dreams. Welcome it with fearless intention. Build on it, no matter how uncertain it may seem. Count on the Spirit to aid you in the makings and workings of your heart. Champion your very best future! Dare to make a brand new start!

Anew!

REFLECTION QUESTION

What unprecedented version of your life
will be revealed with the launch of your new year?

WEEK 3

Anew!

My New Year is My New Norm that Catapults My Unprecedented Future!

Day 2

CENTER

How does this week's reading CENTER me and bring calm, balance, and breathing space to my worldview?

Day 3

CALL

How does this week's reading CALL to me? How am I being awakened with a greater sense of purpose and spirituality? How am I inspired to be a force for good in the world?

Day 4

CHALLENGE

How does this week's reading CHALLENGE me to grow? What am I now ready to adjust, release, forgive, and accept as a result of this week's reading?

WEEK

3

Day 5 **CLARITY**

What new CLARITY have I gained as a result of this week's reading? What better understanding do I now possess?

Day 6 **COMFORT**

What brings me COMFORT about this week's reading? How am I more at ease or consoled by this week's reading?

Day 7 **CHANGE**

How am I CHANGED by this week's reading? What insights, transforming thoughts, inner realizations, overcomings and breakthroughs am I now experiencing?

Anger

I AM liberated by my anger, not imprisoned by it.

"No. Not even as small as an atom. Or maybe a nucleus of an atom. Or maybe a proton. Or maybe a quark."

—Malala's response on being asked if she was angry after being shot in the face by the Taliban

Whether it be a burning inferno or a smoldering ember, anger is the defensive emotional mechanism that bites, burns, snaps, devours, and wards against any perceived offense or injustice aimed at the soft, sensitive spaces of the soul.

What is lesser known about anger, is that it is a creative force and holds tremendous power for good. In its unharnessed, untrained, and underdeveloped form, it is toxic, counterproductive and destructive. Whether it is passive grudge-holding or aggressive hate speech, anger must be guided by a Higher Power in order to produce peace. When anger is used as fuel to fight injustice, save the environment, or power a movement, the energy used to transmute it from a lower toxic frequency to a higher constructive frequency creates peace in the soul and healing on the planet. It's not that the sage doesn't get angry, she never lets her anger get the best of her.

Anger

REFLECTION QUESTION

How can your anger
be used to create the change you wish to see?

Anger

I AM liberated by my anger, not imprisoned by it

Day 2

CENTER

How does this week's reading CENTER me and bring calm, balance, and breathing space to my worldview?

Day 3

CALL

How does this week's reading CALL to me? How am I being awakened with a greater sense of purpose and spirituality? How am I inspired to be a force for good in the world?

Day 4

CHALLENGE

How does this week's reading CHALLENGE me to grow? What am I now ready to adjust, release, forgive, and accept as a result of this week's reading?

Day 5 **CLARITY**

What new CLARITY have I gained as a result of this week's reading? What better understanding do I now possess?

Day 6 **COMFORT**

What brings me COMFORT about this week's reading? How am I more at ease or consoled by this week's reading?

Day 7 **CHANGE**

How am I CHANGED by this week's reading? What insights, transforming thoughts, inner realizations, overcomings and breakthroughs am I now experiencing?

Answers

I ask better questions as I gain clarity about the answers I seek.

"The uncreative mind can spot wrong answers, but it takes a very creative mind to spot wrong questions."

— Antony Jay

Many people spend much of their lives looking for answers. We all have experienced times when answers seem fleeting, and difficult to find. But if answers are hard to come by, perhaps it is because we are searching in the wrong place or looking in the wrong direction.

Spiritually speaking, answers occur through a corresponding partnership with questions. It is through the curious exploration and embrace of questions that information is obtained and answers are found. That being the case, if we haven't found the answer we are looking for, perhaps we have not asked the right question.

Relax. Breathe. Become still, knowing that the answers you are in search of indeed exist. Pleasantly be with a question that corresponds with the answers you seek. Enjoy the mystery it presents. Be open to the Universal aid that may come as an idea, an insight, an inkling or a notion. What comes to you may not be the answer, but may lead to a better question. Good questions lead to great answers.

REFLECTION QUESTION

What question, if answered,
would lead me to the discovery of my deepest desire and
the fulfillment of my greatest dream?

Answers

I ask better questions as I gain clarity about the answers I seek.

Day 2

CENTER

How does this week's reading CENTER me and bring calm, balance, and breathing space to my worldview?

Day 3

CALL

How does this week's reading CALL to me? How am I being awakened with a greater sense of purpose and spirituality? How am I inspired to be a force for good in the world?

Day 4

CHALLENGE

How does this week's reading CHALLENGE me to grow? What am I now ready to adjust, release, forgive, and accept as a result of this week's reading?

WEEK

5

Day 5 **CLARITY**

What new CLARITY have I gained as a result of this week's reading? What better understanding do I now possess?

Day 6 **COMFORT**

What brings me COMFORT about this week's reading? How am I more at ease or consoled by this week's reading?

Day 7 **CHANGE**

How am I CHANGED by this week's reading? What insights, transforming thoughts, inner realizations, overcomings and breakthroughs am I now experiencing?

There is something in every one of you that waits and listens for the sound of the genuine in yourself. It is the only true guide you will ever have. And if you cannot hear it, you will all of your life spend your days on the ends of strings that somebody else pulls."

—Howard Thurman

I behold the beauty in everyone and in everything!

"Never lose an opportunity of seeing anything beautiful, for beauty is God's handwriting."

— Ralph Waldo Emerson

Rampant throughout all creation is a specialness that makes a thing, a thing or a person, a person, or a place, a place - distinct from all other things, and persons, and places. This specialness is the quality of beauty. Beauty is the evidence that within the Universe there is sacred intention encoded within all of creation and for all of life and all things in existence to be held in awe, celebrated and adored.

The Creator paints the sky with an amber and grapefruit colored sunset so that all seeing may pause and appreciate the specialness of the light that brightens the day. Beauty is also found in the seamlessness of a process. The rooting down of the acorn, the birthing of trunk and bark, the sprouting and rising of the fully-leaved majestic oak. This all holds a specialness called beauty. Nothing is more breathtaking than to experience the beauty of the soul. It can be captured in his laugh, in the striking features of her cheek bones, or in the gentleness of their way. Indeed, beauty is the mother of appreciation.

REFLECTION QUESTION

What beauty are you present to right now? And in what way will you acknowledge it?

WEEK 6

I behold the beauty in everyone and in everything!

Day 2

CENTER

How does this week's reading CENTER me and bring calm, balance, and breathing space to my worldview?

Day 3

CALL

How does this week's reading CALL to me? How am I being awakened with a greater sense of purpose and spirituality? How am I inspired to be a force for good in the world?

Day 4

CHALLENGE

How does this week's reading CHALLENGE me to grow? What am I now ready to adjust, release, forgive, and accept as a result of this week's reading?

WEEK 6

Day 5 **CLARITY**

What new CLARITY have I gained as a result of this week's reading? What better understanding do I now possess?

Day 6 **COMFORT**

What brings me COMFORT about this week's reading? How am I more at ease or consoled by this week's reading?

Day 7 **CHANGE**

How am I CHANGED by this week's reading? What insights, transforming thoughts, inner realizations, overcomings and breakthroughs am I now experiencing?

I AM guided and guarded by safe spaces that receive me as I AM.

"Sometimes you want to go where everybody knows your name and they're always glad you came."

– Theme Song to the hit TV show "Cheers"

At least once in every human experience, a soul feels as if it is an outsider and does not belong. Whether not being picked for the softball team by schoolyard playmates, not being admitted to a fraternity or sorority that you pledge for with all your heart, being rejected by a love interest, or living with the crushing embarrassment of being evicted from a place you called home, belonging is a spiritual urge within the soul of each person. It is the "longing" to "be" one with all of life. It is such a compelling impulse within humans that in the absence of healthy, safe, affirming spaces to belong, people willingly choose unhealthy, dangerous, and even deadly places to belong.

Each soul that enters the planet arrives through a custom-made safe space that was fashioned exclusively for nurturing life, building strength, fostering growth, and cultivating health. That place where we experience that deep sense of belonging is called home. It is Life's first gift to us. Recreating this experience for ourselves and for others is our gift back to Life. Strive to remember this place called home and take it wherever you go. It's in so doing that you will find yourself a stranger to no one and friend to the world.

REFLECTION QUESTION

Whose face and name comes to mind
when you consider those that have created a sense of
belonging for you and why?

WEEK 7

Belong

I AM guided and guarded by safe spaces that receive me as I AM.

Day 2

CENTER

How does this week's reading CENTER me and bring calm, balance, and breathing space to my worldview?

Day 3

CALL

How does this week's reading CALL to me? How am I being awakened with a greater sense of purpose and spirituality? How am I inspired to be a force for good in the world?

Day 4

CHALLENGE

How does this week's reading CHALLENGE me to grow? What am I now ready to adjust, release, forgive, and accept as a result of this week's reading?

WEEK 7

Day 5

CLARITY

What new CLARITY have I gained as a result of this week's reading? What better understanding do I now possess?

Day 6

COMFORT

What brings me COMFORT about this week's reading? How am I more at ease or consoled by this week's reading?

Day 7

CHANGE

How am I CHANGED by this week's reading? What insights, transforming thoughts, inner realizations, overcomings and breakthroughs am I now experiencing?

I yield to the impulse of Spirit and say "yes" to the high call of service for my life.

"Everybody can be great because anybody can serve. You only need a heart full of love and a soul generated by grace."

— The Reverend Dr. Martin Luther King, Jr.

Every soul has an assignment and every path leads to the moment of truth when your thirst for fulfillment meets with a higher call to serve. Every time this moment comes for you, throw your heart wide open and shout to your higher power, "CHOOSE ME! USE ME!" Take confidence in knowing that answering the call to serve initiates your date with destiny. Then stand ready and open your eyes, ears and hands and witness as the winds of providence sweep you into the skies of purpose. It is in soaring in the sacred skies of purpose that your name will be etched in the fertile grounds of greatness.

Choose Me! Use Me!

REFLECTION QUESTION

What soul journey are you
prepared to take in service to your higher calling?

WEEK 8

Choose Me! Use Me!

I yield to the impulse of Spirit and say "yes" to the high call of service for my life.

Day 2 **CENTER**

How does this week's reading CENTER me and bring calm, balance, and breathing space to my worldview?

Day 3 **CALL**

How does this week's reading CALL to me? How am I being awakened with a greater sense of purpose and spirituality? How am I inspired to be a force for good in the world?

Day 4 **CHALLENGE**

How does this week's reading CHALLENGE me to grow? What am I now ready to adjust, release, forgive, and accept as a result of this week's reading?

WEEK
8

Day 5 **CLARITY**

What new CLARITY have I gained as a result of this week's reading? What better understanding do I now possess?

Day 6 **COMFORT**

What brings me COMFORT about this week's reading? How am I more at ease or consoled by this week's reading?

Day 7 **CHANGE**

How am I CHANGED by this week's reading? What insights, transforming thoughts, inner realizations, overcomings and breakthroughs am I now experiencing?

Connect

I have the ability to connect, to love, to live, to give and to forgive, and I use my talents for that purpose.

"The greatness of a man is not in how much wealth he acquires, but in his integrity and his ability to affect those around him positively."

— Bob Marley

Renown singer and actress Della Reese, who I admire very much for her voice and her talent, shared with an audience what helped her reach the top when her talent and artistry was not enough. She noticed that while she had the ability to hit all the notes, her mentor Mahalia Jackson possessed a skill that carried her far beyond the music. Mahalia's genius was her ability to connect with those she sang to.

We all have abilities that when put to use, are impressive. However, becoming clear about the purpose our talents are used for can be the difference between a talent and a gift. We all can use our talents and skills to connect, to love, to live, to give and forgive.

Connect

REFLECTION QUESTION

How can I connect
with others as I share the talents and skills I possess?

WEEK 9

Connect

I have the ability to connect, to love, to live, to give and to forgive, and I use my talents for that purpose.

Day 2

CENTER

How does this week's reading CENTER me and bring calm, balance, and breathing space to my worldview?

Day 3

CALL

How does this week's reading CALL to me? How am I being awakened with a greater sense of purpose and spirituality? How am I inspired to be a force for good in the world?

Day 4

CHALLENGE

How does this week's reading CHALLENGE me to grow? What am I now ready to adjust, release, forgive, and accept as a result of this week's reading?

WEEK

9

Day 5 **CLARITY**

What new CLARITY have I gained as a result of this week's reading? What better understanding do I now possess?

Day 6 **COMFORT**

What brings me COMFORT about this week's reading? How am I more at ease or consoled by this week's reading?

Day 7 **CHANGE**

How am I CHANGED by this week's reading? What insights, transforming thoughts, inner realizations, overcomings and breakthroughs am I now experiencing?

"Our goal should be to live life in radical amazement. ...get up in the morning and look at the world in a way that takes nothing for granted. Everything is phenomenal; everything is incredible; never treat life casually. To be spiritual is to be amazed."

—Rabbi Abraham Joshua Heschel

I take time to move joyously in celebration of life and in the opportunity for expression and growth.

"Dance is the hidden language of the soul."

— Martha Graham

There are many reasons why people dance. Sometimes we dance for entertainment and pleasure. Other times we dance for exercise and fitness. Dance is also freeing. Dancing helps us release cares and concerns, and cope with the rigors brought on by the day.

From a deeper level, dancing can mirror life. Sometimes we lead, and other times we are led. Sometimes even our toes are stepped on. But ultimately, dancing allows us to keep "in step" and connected with the rhythm and the pulse of a greater, inner truth that can't always be expressed in words. The courage to step onto the floor in dance can give us the same courage to take the next step in an area of our lives. A twist, turn or spin in dance can inspire us to make a bold move. When watching or participating in a dance, watch what dissolves and what unfolds for you.

Dance

REFLECTION QUESTION

What becomes available for me
when I dance that I can use to effectively move around and
pass through the obstacles in my life?

WEEK 10

I take time to move joyously in celebration of life and in the opportunity for expression and growth.

Day 2 **CENTER**

How does this week's reading CENTER me and bring calm, balance, and breathing space to my worldview?

Day 3 **CALL**

How does this week's reading CALL to me? How am I being awakened with a greater sense of purpose and spirituality? How am I inspired to be a force for good in the world?

Day 4 **CHALLENGE**

How does this week's reading CHALLENGE me to grow? What am I now ready to adjust, release, forgive, and accept as a result of this week's reading?

WEEK

10

Day 5 **CLARITY**

What new CLARITY have I gained as a result of this week's reading? What better understanding do I now possess?

Day 6 **COMFORT**

What brings me COMFORT about this week's reading? How am I more at ease or consoled by this week's reading?

Day 7 **CHANGE**

How am I CHANGED by this week's reading? What insights, transforming thoughts, inner realizations, overcomings and breakthroughs am I now experiencing?

Divine Order

I allow the Holy Spirit to work on my behalf, manifesting every element for my good.

"I trust in the ebb and flow of the universe. I trust that life's bigger than what I can see. I trust that there is a divine order beyond my control. And I trust that no matter what happens, I will be alright."

— Oprah Winfrey

Divine Order is a faith-filled understanding of how things spiritually come into being, and an alignment with the ideal outcome for all concerned. Proclaiming "DIVINE ORDER," is in no way a resignation to whatever happens, nor is Divine Order a surrender to a worrisome situation. It is a *declaration of cooperation* with the outworking of spiritual law. Peace, harmony and happiness is what ultimately results.

Take a moment now to become still and acknowledge the many ways in which order operates in the universe. Pause any impulse to accept short cuts that does not allow for the fullness that comes in time and in season. Affirm, *"I allow the Holy Spirit to work on my behalf, manifesting every element for my good. I am in harmony with all there is, and I am now in perfect peace."*

Divine Order

REFLECTION QUESTION

What experiences have you had or stories can you tell about timely and orderly outcomes?

WEEK 11

Divine Order

I allow the Holy Spirit to work on my behalf, manifesting every element for my good.

Day 2 — CENTER

How does this week's reading CENTER me and bring calm, balance, and breathing space to my worldview?

Day 3 — CALL

How does this week's reading CALL to me? How am I being awakened with a greater sense of purpose and spirituality? How am I inspired to be a force for good in the world?

Day 4 — CHALLENGE

How does this week's reading CHALLENGE me to grow? What am I now ready to adjust, release, forgive, and accept as a result of this week's reading?

WEEK

11

Day 5 **CLARITY**

What new CLARITY have I gained as a result of this week's reading? What better understanding do I now possess?

Day 6 **COMFORT**

What brings me COMFORT about this week's reading? How am I more at ease or consoled by this week's reading?

Day 7 **CHANGE**

How am I CHANGED by this week's reading? What insights, transforming thoughts, inner realizations, overcomings and breakthroughs am I now experiencing?

I open myself to Spirit and the good desires of my heart are rekindled and restored.

"No one's ever completely broken. It's just a matter of how much has to fall apart before the ember of life is exposed to air."

— Charles Eisenstein

There are times in life when it seems that the fire, the enthusiasm and inspiration to continue, is being extinguished. The burning desire to dream cools down and the energy to pursue our goals seem to cool off.

Our souls seem to fatigue as the disappointments of life whittle away at our ambitions. Yet as we turn away from those bitter disappointments, we often find something left; an ember of hope. Embers of this sort are the remnants of our failed efforts. Embers live in the ashes of dreams dashed and unfulfilled, and are dampened in the scattered experiences we left behind. And while their light seems to be smothered and dimmed, all an ember needs is a little fresh air.

If you feel burned out or simply exhausted, take a moment to breathe. Allow the inflow to clear your mind of anything clouding or stifling your God-given desires. Let the Spirit blow and brush away the soot smudging your divine thoughts and ideas. Then, open your heart to the Spirit, and feel the eternal breath restore your soul, renew your strength, refresh your ideas and spark new interest!

Watch as what seemed snuffed out catches fire again. Let your ember's fiery resilience inspire you and its warmth be a reminder of all that remains possible for you.

REFLECTION QUESTION

What embers do you have in your possession that can be rekindled with a little fresh air?

WEEK 12

Embers

I open myself to Spirit and the good desires of my heart are rekindled and restored.

Day 2 — CENTER

How does this week's reading CENTER me and bring calm, balance, and breathing space to my worldview?

____

____

____

____

Day 3 — CALL

How does this week's reading CALL to me? How am I being awakened with a greater sense of purpose and spirituality? How am I inspired to be a force for good in the world?

____

____

____

____

Day 4 — CHALLENGE

How does this week's reading CHALLENGE me to grow? What am I now ready to adjust, release, forgive, and accept as a result of this week's reading?

____

____

____

____

WEEK

12

Day 5 **CLARITY**

What new CLARITY have I gained as a result of this week's reading? What better understanding do I now possess?

Day 6 **COMFORT**

What brings me COMFORT about this week's reading? How am I more at ease or consoled by this week's reading?

Day 7 **CHANGE**

How am I CHANGED by this week's reading? What insights, transforming thoughts, inner realizations, overcomings and breakthroughs am I now experiencing?

Food

I hold with great reverence the food that fuels my life.

"God is great. God is good. And we thank God for this food. By God's hands we all are fed. Give us Lord our daily bread. Amen"

— Anonymous

Food. The word itself is synonymous with life. Everything about it connects us to what we value most essential about living. Food intersects with family, friends, work, play, health and happiness. It is the universal something that the whole of humanity depends on, and it is that universal dependence upon food that is the great equalizer among men and women. No person's rank, social status, financial position, set of accomplishments, or lack thereof is relevant in its absence, and in its presence, all of life is its vulnerable dependent, irrespective of when or where we encounter it.

Twenty years after my mother insisted that my brothers and I "give thanks" each time we sat at the table to eat, did I come to fully appreciate why she insisted on us developing such a habit. Eating food is a privilege that we must remember not to take for granted. Amidst our work-obsessed, high tech-low touch, instant gratification, drive-thru culture, eating good, healthy, nutritious meals can come as an inconvenience. It slows us down, interrupts our busy lives, and forces us to sit with others and be still. In short, it never fails to do its job. It is when we are sitting still with food that we can take a moment to mindfully acknowledge its journey to our plates. A network of interconnectedness and highly sophisticated relationships play a role in every bite we take. From the seed, the sower, the soil, the water, the weather, the farmer, the fisherman, the trucker, the grocer, the butcher, the baker, the chef and our Creator; a cloud of witnesses are present at every meal. They join us in reverent gratitude for the bounty of the Earth, our connection to it and to each other.

Food

REFLECTION QUESTION

In what ways do you show reverence for food?

WEEK 13

Food

I hold with great reverence the food that fuels my life.

Day 2 **CENTER**

How does this week's reading CENTER me and bring calm, balance, and breathing space to my worldview?

Day 3 **CALL**

How does this week's reading CALL to me? How am I being awakened with a greater sense of purpose and spirituality? How am I inspired to be a force for good in the world?

Day 4 **CHALLENGE**

How does this week's reading CHALLENGE me to grow? What am I now ready to adjust, release, forgive, and accept as a result of this week's reading?

WEEK

13

Day 5 **CLARITY**

What new CLARITY have I gained as a result of this week's reading? What better understanding do I now possess?

Day 6 **COMFORT**

What brings me COMFORT about this week's reading? How am I more at ease or consoled by this week's reading?

Day 7 **CHANGE**

How am I CHANGED by this week's reading? What insights, transforming thoughts, inner realizations, overcomings and breakthroughs am I now experiencing?

"We need to find God, and God cannot be found in noise and restlessness. God is the friend of silence. See how nature – trees, flowers, grass- grows in silence; see the stars, the moon and the sun, how they move in silence... We need silence to be able to touch souls."

—Mother Teresa

Freedom

I am aware of my freedom in God and I am at liberty to make great decisions.

***"There is freedom waiting for you, On the breezes of the sky,
And you ask, "What if I fall?"
Oh but my darling, What if you fly?"***

— Erin Hanson

Within the Energy, Intelligence and Infiniteness we call God, is a freedom and liberation that occurs at our very awareness of Its presence. The feeling is expansive, non-confining and unlimited. The very thought of God frees us of any erring suggestion of lack or limitation. We can make decisions from this consciousness, and express with clarity our potential out of a myriad of possibilities.

Right now, in your mind's eye, begin to see the results of this awareness of God. See your questions answered, your problems dissolving, and your issues resolved. Focus only on what you want; not what you don't want. Allow the Spirit of God to reveal and handle the how. Simply breathe, and in this moment, see the result you seek, unencumbered by any contentious or competing thought. Decide now to freely receive this reality in God with gratitude and joy. Continue to walk in this eye-opening awareness of God's ever-present assistance, making every decision from this truth.

REFLECTION QUESTION

If you had the final word
in any area of your life, what would you say?

WEEK 14

I am aware of my freedom in God and I am at liberty to make great decisions.

Day 2 **CENTER**

How does this week's reading CENTER me and bring calm, balance, and breathing space to my worldview?

Day 3 **CALL**

How does this week's reading CALL to me? How am I being awakened with a greater sense of purpose and spirituality? How am I inspired to be a force for good in the world?

Day 4 **CHALLENGE**

How does this week's reading CHALLENGE me to grow? What am I now ready to adjust, release, forgive, and accept as a result of this week's reading?

Day 5 **CLARITY**

What new CLARITY have I gained as a result of this week's reading? What better understanding do I now possess?

Day 6 **COMFORT**

What brings me COMFORT about this week's reading? How am I more at ease or consoled by this week's reading?

Day 7 **CHANGE**

How am I CHANGED by this week's reading? What insights, transforming thoughts, inner realizations, overcomings and breakthroughs am I now experiencing?

Go

I AM a unique, creative expression of Divinity going somewhere to happen!

"Until one is committed, there is hesitancy, the chance to draw back, always ineffectiveness. Concerning all acts of initiative and creation, this is one elementary truth the ignorance of which kills countless ideas and splendid plans; that the moment one definitely commits oneself, then Providence moves too."

— William Hutchinson Murray

At some point, it must happen. The "it" of which I speak is the removal of the gear from neutral and the foot from the proverbial brake of life. At some point, we must come out of the "getting-ready-to-get-ready" closet of prolonged procrastination. At some point, we lift our eyes from the plan and move our minds from the abyss of analysis paralysis and we must work our plans. No amount of preparation can substitute for what you learn by taking definite action.

Go is the two-letter word that breaks through all of the mental, emotional, and physical red tape that separates us from experiencing the full expression of our potential. No big dreams can be materialized. No great humanitarian solutions can be discovered. No new exciting enterprises can be launched until someone dares to "go." Go and find the love of your life. Go and get your college degree. Go and challenge injustice. Go and wage peace amidst the conflict. Go sing your song, dance your dance, unveil your art. By all means, just go! We go so that the trails in our own minds don't become overrun with the weeds of excuse, regret, procrastination, self-doubt, self-pity, blame and shame. We go in order to evolve our souls, reveal and reflect the Presence of Divinity, and to be a force for good in the world.

Go

REFLECTION QUESTION

What mental, emotional, physical and spiritual weeds must be excavated in order for you to feel fully free to go and be your best self?

WEEK 15

Go

I AM a unique, creative expression of Divinity going somewhere to happen!

Day 2 CENTER

How does this week's reading CENTER me and bring calm, balance, and breathing space to my worldview?

____

____

____

____

Day 3 CALL

How does this week's reading CALL to me? How am I being awakened with a greater sense of purpose and spirituality? How am I inspired to be a force for good in the world?

____

____

____

____

Day 4 CHALLENGE

How does this week's reading CHALLENGE me to grow? What am I now ready to adjust, release, forgive, and accept as a result of this week's reading?

____

____

____

____

WEEK 15

Day 5 — CLARITY

What new CLARITY have I gained as a result of this week's reading? What better understanding do I now possess?

Day 6 — COMFORT

What brings me COMFORT about this week's reading? How am I more at ease or consoled by this week's reading?

Day 7 — CHANGE

How am I CHANGED by this week's reading? What insights, transforming thoughts, inner realizations, overcomings and breakthroughs am I now experiencing?

Harmony

I seek to live my life harmoniously with others as we join together in a common key.

"The key to world harmony is for everyone to be on a chord."

— Eric Ovid Donaldson

Music can teach us a lot about how to live together peacefully with one another. To live harmoniously is to find compatibility in any activity of the moment; to be in-sync and seek agreement with those around you as though a song is being sung or music is being made.

Living life in harmony with others takes a willingness to find a common key to play in. It also requires sound arrangements, good timing, and a listening ear for what others are contributing toward its fit and finish.

The music in my mind has a unifying quality. It brings people together and easily accepts them into a chorale of kindness. As I breathe, I find my rhythm, and my soul sings gleefully and gloriously with others.

REFLECTION QUESTION

How are others instrumental in your life, and what songs titles are playing on your personal life soundtrack?

I seek to live my life harmoniously with others as we join together in a common key.

Day 2 **CENTER**

How does this week's reading CENTER me and bring calm, balance, and breathing space to my worldview?

Day 3 **CALL**

How does this week's reading CALL to me? How am I being awakened with a greater sense of purpose and spirituality? How am I inspired to be a force for good in the world?

Day 4 **CHALLENGE**

How does this week's reading CHALLENGE me to grow? What am I now ready to adjust, release, forgive, and accept as a result of this week's reading?

WEEK

16

Day 5 **CLARITY**

What new CLARITY have I gained as a result of this week's reading? What better understanding do I now possess?

Day 6 **COMFORT**

What brings me COMFORT about this week's reading? How am I more at ease or consoled by this week's reading?

Day 7 **CHANGE**

How am I CHANGED by this week's reading? What insights, transforming thoughts, inner realizations, overcomings and breakthroughs am I now experiencing?

I AM a joyous channel of celebration, jubilation and fun!

"One seems to hear words of good cheer from everywhere filling the air."

—"Carol of the Bells" by John Williams

The wafts of our favorite dish thick in the air, the outburst of surprise by familiar faces reuniting, the loud talk of grown folks who gather in the foyer, the racing screech of little ones whizzing by, the blare of the brassy tunes, the parade of larger than life cartoons, the sparkle of well strewn tinsel, the colorful clothes and costumes and the cozy fire, all to join family and friends together in sacred remembrance of that special day. Be it a birthday or wedding, baby shower, or baptism, we all have our way to mark that break in time. A break from the busyness. A pause from duty. A relief from reporting. A time for celebration. For some it's Eid, or Christmas, Hanukkah or New Year's Eve, Kwanzaa or Diwali, it's the memories we relive. For some it's Mardi Gras or Festivus, Easter or Indigenous People's Day. Whatever people call it. We all know it to be play.

So breath in the excitement. Feast to your heart's content. Laugh till your sides ache. Relish the merriment. Dance 'till it's sunrise. Sing though it be off key. Cherish every story, make them new memories. Pray in the stillness. Remember the Sacred One. Just as there's time for business, know there's also time for having fun.

REFLECTION QUESTION

What's the next cause for celebration in your life?

I AM a joyous channel of celebration, jubilation and fun!

Day 2 **CENTER**

How does this week's reading CENTER me and bring calm, balance, and breathing space to my worldview?

____

____

____

____

Day 3 **CALL**

How does this week's reading CALL to me? How am I being awakened with a greater sense of purpose and spirituality? How am I inspired to be a force for good in the world?

____

____

____

____

Day 4 **CHALLENGE**

How does this week's reading CHALLENGE me to grow? What am I now ready to adjust, release, forgive, and accept as a result of this week's reading?

____

____

____

____

WEEK

17

Day 5 **CLARITY**

What new CLARITY have I gained as a result of this week's reading? What better understanding do I now possess?

Day 6 **COMFORT**

What brings me COMFORT about this week's reading? How am I more at ease or consoled by this week's reading?

Day 7 **CHANGE**

How am I CHANGED by this week's reading? What insights, transforming thoughts, inner realizations, overcomings and breakthroughs am I now experiencing?

"Flowers do not force their way with great strife. Flowers open to perfection slowly in the sun. . . . Don't be in a hurry about spiritual matters. Go step by step, and be very sure."

—White Eagle

Horizons

I lift my eyes toward that which lies just beyond the horizon, and faithfully step in the direction of my dreams.

"A dream is the bearer of a new possibility, the enlarged horizon, the great hope."

— Howard Thurman

The power of a horizon lies in its ability to signal the arrival of something new and to bring closure to that which is complete.

Hopes, goals and dreams lie on this horizon, and more clearly come into our view as we dutifully take the steps necessary to move toward them. Horizons serve as departure points as well. Things that have served its purpose, or are moving toward its next chapter fade into the distance or become a distant memory as it too solemnly settles into the horizon.

As you meditate today, set your spiritual sights on the horizon. In your mind's eye, welcome a beautiful, breathtaking sunrise as it sheds light upon all of the good the day will bring you. Then breathe a refreshing sigh of relief and release, as the sun sets, and takes the toils of the day with it. Know that all is well, and that space is now made for new horizons.

Horizons

REFLECTION QUESTION

As you look toward your horizons, what possibilities do you see emerging? What areas in your life are coming to a close?

I lift my eyes toward that which lies just beyond the horizon, and faithfully step in the direction of my dreams.

Day 2

CENTER

How does this week's reading CENTER me and bring calm, balance, and breathing space to my worldview?

Day 3

CALL

How does this week's reading CALL to me? How am I being awakened with a greater sense of purpose and spirituality? How am I inspired to be a force for good in the world?

Day 4

CHALLENGE

How does this week's reading CHALLENGE me to grow? What am I now ready to adjust, release, forgive, and accept as a result of this week's reading?

WEEK

18

Day 5 CLARITY

What new CLARITY have I gained as a result of this week's reading? What better understanding do I now possess?

Day 6 COMFORT

What brings me COMFORT about this week's reading? How am I more at ease or consoled by this week's reading?

Day 7 CHANGE

How am I CHANGED by this week's reading? What insights, transforming thoughts, inner realizations, overcomings and breakthroughs am I now experiencing?

Impressions

I am committed to my unique spiritual expression leaving a beautiful and indelible impression upon all I meet and encounter.

"The purpose of life is not to be happy. It is to be useful, to be honorable, to be compassionate, to have it make some difference that you have lived and lived well."

— Ralph Waldo Emerson

You may have heard it said that we are one in the Spirit. We are also unique, individualized expressions of the Spirit, given an opportunity to make a good and meaningful impression. Take for example, a fresh covering of snow. Each flake of snow looks the same on the surface, yet differs the closer we look. Each snowflake carries an intricate unique pattern; no two are the same. God makes spiritual impressions—wonderful ways in which Spirit works in, through, and as ourselves. And no one in the world can express exactly as you do!

I effectively express the goodness of God through the power of Love. First, I love God, the animating Presence and Power that moves and inspires my soul. Next, I love myself; the creation that the Supreme Creator wonderfully made. Finally, I find ways and opportunities to express love to and for all, using the gifts and talents God gives me. What a beautiful way to leave unique and lasting impressions that reflect the glory of God.

Impressions

REFLECTION QUESTION

In what ways am I
uniquely equipped to bless and impress those I encounter?

WEEK 19

Impressions

I am committed to my unique Spiritual expression leaving a beautiful and indelible impression upon all I meet and encounter.

Day 2 — CENTER

How does this week's reading CENTER me and bring calm, balance, and breathing space to my worldview?

____

____

____

____

Day 3 — CALL

How does this week's reading CALL to me? How am I being awakened with a greater sense of purpose and spirituality? How am I inspired to be a force for good in the world?

____

____

____

____

Day 4 — CHALLENGE

How does this week's reading CHALLENGE me to grow? What am I now ready to adjust, release, forgive, and accept as a result of this week's reading?

____

____

____

____

WEEK

19

Day 5 CLARITY

What new CLARITY have I gained as a result of this week's reading? What better understanding do I now possess?

Day 6 COMFORT

What brings me COMFORT about this week's reading? How am I more at ease or consoled by this week's reading?

Day 7 CHANGE

How am I CHANGED by this week's reading? What insights, transforming thoughts, inner realizations, overcomings and breakthroughs am I now experiencing?

I AM a distribution channel of courageous compassion that leads to justice!

"Justice is what love looks like in public."

— Dr. Cornell West

There are names that when invoked, are immediately synonymous with the experience of injustice. George Floyd, for instance, suffered an unimaginable modern day lynching, as the world watched a sworn law enforcement officer kneel on his neck, for eight minutes and forty six seconds until he died. During the moments leading to his demise, he begged for his breath and finally for his "Mama." And the world got to see for itself, the tremendous injustice that countless numbers of unarmed Black men and women have been suffering at the hands of bad actors in law enforcement all across America for centuries. Something about this moment, however, was different than previous flash points in our nation's history, because people were forced to look at the undeniable darkness within society and within themselves and make a choice.

Finding safe sacred spaces to process through the anger, rage, pain, and grief that accompanies exposure to societal injustice, will furnish us with the clarity we need to emerge better, not bitter. If there is any benefit to witnessing injustice, it is this. It is the opportunity to answer the question, *"Now that I am aware that this exists, who do I choose to be in its face?"* Justice, therefore, is the selfless product of people who choose public displays of courageous compassion in an effort to grant, even the so-called, "least of these" an equal share of benefit at the table of humanity.

Justice

REFLECTION QUESTION

In what ways has your journey prompted you to display courageous compassion on behalf of those experiencing injustice?

WEEK 20

Justice

I AM a distribution channel of courageous compassion that leads to justice!

Day 2

CENTER

How does this week's reading CENTER me and bring calm, balance, and breathing space to my worldview?

Day 3

CALL

How does this week's reading CALL to me? How am I being awakened with a greater sense of purpose and spirituality? How am I inspired to be a force for good in the world?

Day 4

CHALLENGE

How does this week's reading CHALLENGE me to grow? What am I now ready to adjust, release, forgive, and accept as a result of this week's reading?

WEEK 20

Day 5 **CLARITY**

What new CLARITY have I gained as a result of this week's reading? What better understanding do I now possess?

Day 6 **COMFORT**

What brings me COMFORT about this week's reading? How am I more at ease or consoled by this week's reading?

Day 7 **CHANGE**

How am I CHANGED by this week's reading? What insights, transforming thoughts, inner realizations, overcomings and breakthroughs am I now experiencing?

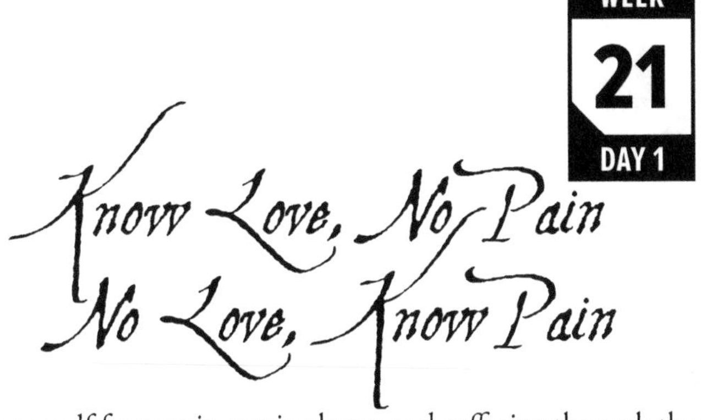
Know Love, No Pain
No Love, Know Pain

I free myself from pain, panic, shame and suffering through the liberating power of Divine Love!

"There is no difficulty that enough love will not conquer: no disease that love will not heal: no door that enough love will not open...It makes no difference how deep set the trouble: how hopeless the outlook: how muddled the tangle: how great the mistake. A sufficient realization of love will dissolve it all. If only you could love enough you would be the happiest and most powerful being in the world..."

— Emmet Fox

Most people in pain use anger to cover it, fear to avoid it, jealousy to deflect it, violence to protect it and cosmetics to conceal it. While life's painful experiences create discomfort and some unhappiness, it is not your permanent foe. Pain is information that has arrived in your life under grace, to alert you that a necessary adjustment needs to be made. As you seek to heal what pains you, know that the absence of love will prolong the pain and the presence of Divine love will dissolve it.

Today choose to gently, but liberally apply Divine love, as a healing salve to the hurting, broken, and bitter places and spaces in your life by taking easy deep breaths. Connect to this great love and feel the whole and Holy Spirit wash over you. Let It guide you to make the right adjustment away from resentment to forgiveness, from shame to self-love, from fear to courage, and from bondage to freedom. Remember you are one holy breath away from the pain into the peace of Divine Love.

Know Love, No Pain
No Love, Know Pain

REFLECTION QUESTION

What pain is there in your life that is
calling for Divine Love to dissolve it and set you free?

WEEK 21

Know Love, No Pain
No Love, Know Pain

I free myself from pain, panic, shame and suffering through the liberating power of Divine Love!

Day 2

CENTER

How does this week's reading CENTER me and bring calm, balance, and breathing space to my worldview?

____

____

____

____

Day 3

CALL

How does this week's reading CALL to me? How am I being awakened with a greater sense of purpose and spirituality? How am I inspired to be a force for good in the world?

____

____

____

____

Day 4

CHALLENGE

How does this week's reading CHALLENGE me to grow? What am I now ready to adjust, release, forgive, and accept as a result of this week's reading?

____

____

____

____

WEEK

21

Day 5 **CLARITY**

What new CLARITY have I gained as a result of this week's reading? What better understanding do I now possess?

Day 6 **COMFORT**

What brings me COMFORT about this week's reading? How am I more at ease or consoled by this week's reading?

Day 7 **CHANGE**

How am I CHANGED by this week's reading? What insights, transforming thoughts, inner realizations, overcomings and breakthroughs am I now experiencing?

WEEK 21

Know Love, No Pain
No Love, Know Pain

I free myself from pain, panic, shame and suffering through the liberating power of Divine Love!

Day 2

CENTER

How does this week's reading CENTER me and bring calm, balance, and breathing space to my worldview?

Day 3

CALL

How does this week's reading CALL to me? How am I being awakened with a greater sense of purpose and spirituality? How am I inspired to be a force for good in the world?

Day 4

CHALLENGE

How does this week's reading CHALLENGE me to grow? What am I now ready to adjust, release, forgive, and accept as a result of this week's reading?

WEEK

21

Day 5 **CLARITY**

What new CLARITY have I gained as a result of this week's reading? What better understanding do I now possess?

Day 6 **COMFORT**

What brings me COMFORT about this week's reading? How am I more at ease or consoled by this week's reading?

Day 7 **CHANGE**

How am I CHANGED by this week's reading? What insights, transforming thoughts, inner realizations, overcomings and breakthroughs am I now experiencing?

I give a hand-up with what I choose to pass down.

"Legacy is not leaving something for people. It's leaving something in people."

— Peter Strople

How we live our lives today can determine how life is lived tomorrow. As we live life with intention, we can create the legacy we wish to leave others.

How can I be remembered? It can be through a family business I leave, property I bequeath, material and capital gains I will. It can also be through ideals and stories I share, or values and ways of being I embody. To be remembered for our kindness, compassion, and other uplifting and inspiring attributes is a worthy purpose to pursue. Individually or collectively, we add to whatever we choose to leave as a legacy with every choice and decision we make today. Given thoughtfulness and prayer, we all can create legacies that benefit others for generations to come.

REFLECTION QUESTION

What have I done today that
people will gratefully speak about tomorrow?

WEEK 22

I will give a hand-up with what I choose to pass down.

Day 2 **CENTER**

How does this week's reading CENTER me and bring calm, balance, and breathing space to my worldview?

____

____

____

____

Day 3 **CALL**

How does this week's reading CALL to me? How am I being awakened with a greater sense of purpose and spirituality? How am I inspired to be a force for good in the world?

____

____

____

____

Day 4 **CHALLENGE**

How does this week's reading CHALLENGE me to grow? What am I now ready to adjust, release, forgive, and accept as a result of this week's reading?

____

____

____

____

WEEK

22

Day 5 **CLARITY**

What new CLARITY have I gained as a result of this week's reading? What better understanding do I now possess?

Day 6 **COMFORT**

What brings me COMFORT about this week's reading? How am I more at ease or consoled by this week's reading?

Day 7 **CHANGE**

How am I CHANGED by this week's reading? What insights, transforming thoughts, inner realizations, overcomings and breakthroughs am I now experiencing?

"Each one has to find his peace from within. And peace to be real must be unaffected by outside circumstances."
—Mahatma Gandhi

Little Things

I pay careful attention to the little things that hold great significance.

"Upon tiny hinges, swing mighty doors."
— Lawrence E. Carter, Sr.

Many of the great thought leaders throughout history have urged students of success to "think big." While this has served as the catalyst for many great accomplishments, it is not the only thinking required for success. Every great success, every great fortune and every great person hangs the doors to the entrance of their bright future on the tiny hinges of right thinking, self-discipline, consistency, and kindness. While they may seem like little things, they hold great significance and are the building blocks for the consciousness, character, and courage required to maintain success.

Today choose to make a big deal about the little things and the little things will make you a big deal!

REFLECTION QUESTION

What little things in your life are being overlooked and what would be possible for you if you prioritize them today?

WEEK 23

I pay careful attention to the little things that hold great significance.

Day 2

CENTER

How does this week's reading CENTER me and bring calm, balance, and breathing space to my worldview?

Day 3

CALL

How does this week's reading CALL to me? How am I being awakened with a greater sense of purpose and spirituality? How am I inspired to be a force for good in the world?

Day 4

CHALLENGE

How does this week's reading CHALLENGE me to grow? What am I now ready to adjust, release, forgive, and accept as a result of this week's reading?

WEEK

23

Day 5 **CLARITY**

What new CLARITY have I gained as a result of this week's reading? What better understanding do I now possess?

Day 6 **COMFORT**

What brings me COMFORT about this week's reading? How am I more at ease or consoled by this week's reading?

Day 7 **CHANGE**

How am I CHANGED by this week's reading? What insights, transforming thoughts, inner realizations, overcomings and breakthroughs am I now experiencing?

Mastery

I experience the full benefit of my gifts and talents as I operate them with confidence and Mastery.

"It matters not how strait the gate. How charged with punishments the scroll, I am the master of my fate. I am the captain of my soul."

— Invictus by William Ernest Henley

There exists just there in the pit of the stomach a knowingness, a certainty, an immovable grip of assurance that we all recognize when we are operating in an area of our mastery. Whether it be the Grandmother in the kitchen, making her famous peach cobbler. Or the doctor in the operating room, leading life-saving surgery. Or the musical director of a Broadway play, wailing her hands conducting the orchestra. Or the Olympic figure skater, entertaining the world with death defying feats. Or how about the server at the busy restaurant wowing customers with exceptional hospitality?

Mastery is a dance of collaboration that fuses our gifts, skills, and talents with passion, preparation, discipline and that mystical moment in time. As we tap into the deep dimensions of ourselves that unlock our artistry, creativity, ingenuity and our inner genius, and we employ these gifts in service to the world, we have permission to shine!

Mastery

REFLECTION QUESTION

What is your zone of Mastery
and what part of the world shines more brightly because of it?

WEEK
24

Mastery

I experience the full benefit of my gifts and talents as I operate them with confidence and Mastery.

Day 2

CENTER

How does this week's reading CENTER me and bring calm, balance, and breathing space to my worldview?

Day 3

CALL

How does this week's reading CALL to me? How am I being awakened with a greater sense of purpose and spirituality? How am I inspired to be a force for good in the world?

Day 4

CHALLENGE

How does this week's reading CHALLENGE me to grow? What am I now ready to adjust, release, forgive, and accept as a result of this week's reading?

WEEK

24

Day 5 **CLARITY**

What new CLARITY have I gained as a result of this week's reading? What better understanding do I now possess?

Day 6 **COMFORT**

What brings me COMFORT about this week's reading? How am I more at ease or consoled by this week's reading?

Day 7 **CHANGE**

How am I CHANGED by this week's reading? What insights, transforming thoughts, inner realizations, overcomings and breakthroughs am I now experiencing?

Mother

I AM a better soul because of the best I received from my Mother.

"God could not be everywhere and therefore God made mothers."

— Rudyard Kigpling

In all shapes, colors, and forms, from all countries, known and obscure, not a single soul would inhabit the Earth, were it not for our Mothers for sure. Sweet ones, sour ones, weak ones, power ones. Short ones, mean ones. Little and in-between ones. Big ones, tall ones. Plump ones, small ones. Near ones, far ones. Church ones, bar ones.

Happy ones, sad ones. Good ones, bad ones. Adopted ones, birth ones. Strong ones, hurt ones. Healed ones, harmed ones. City ones, farm ones. Night ones, day ones. Freed ones, enslaved ones. Earth ones, heaven ones. Broken down and together ones.

Yes ones. No ones. Fast ones. Slow ones. Fancy ones, plain ones. Bold ones. Afraid ones. Forgiven and blamed ones. Proud and ashamed ones. We can never forget what her name was or what the mention of it does. For living souls like you and I, whose Mother's love is why we dare to fly.

Mother

REFLECTION QUESTION

What quality about your Mother
moves you to become the best version of yourself?

WEEK 25

Mother

I AM a better soul because of the best I received from my Mother.

Day 2 — CENTER

How does this week's reading CENTER me and bring calm, balance, and breathing space to my worldview?

Day 3 — CALL

How does this week's reading CALL to me? How am I being awakened with a greater sense of purpose and spirituality? How am I inspired to be a force for good in the world?

Day 4 — CHALLENGE

How does this week's reading CHALLENGE me to grow? What am I now ready to adjust, release, forgive, and accept as a result of this week's reading?

WEEK 25

Day 5 **CLARITY**

What new CLARITY have I gained as a result of this week's reading? What better understanding do I now possess?

Day 6 **COMFORT**

What brings me COMFORT about this week's reading? How am I more at ease or consoled by this week's reading?

Day 7 **CHANGE**

How am I CHANGED by this week's reading? What insights, transforming thoughts, inner realizations, overcomings and breakthroughs am I now experiencing?

No

I maintain healthy boundaries in my life by saying "no" when I mean "no."

"No is still a complete sentence."

— Kevin Kitrell Ross

No. While it is a simple two letter word, it holds tremendous power to affect our lives. Simply, it is the one word that denies access to any thought, anything, or anyone who wishes to occupy, possess, or obtain our attention, space or property. As simple as this word is to pronounce, saying it out loud or to ourselves inwardly, can present a big struggle. We struggle with saying no mostly because we all want to be liked and rejecting someone's request risks losing their approval. We struggle with saying no to ourselves because we are often driven by the appetites and demands of our senses and the fleeting pleasures they provide.

The good news is, as we exercise our power to say no, we construct healthy boundaries that lead to balance, self-respect, and lasting peace of mind. Saying no frees us to pursue our purest interests, deepest desires and express ourselves in a most authentic way. Ultimately, as we build confidence in saying no, we also build the habit of choosing that which is for our highest good and greatest joy.

No

REFLECTION QUESTION

With whom and under what
circumstances do you struggle with saying no?

WEEK 26

No

I maintain healthy boundaries in my life by saying "no" when I mean "no."

Day 2

CENTER

How does this week's reading CENTER me and bring calm, balance, and breathing space to my worldview?

Day 3

CALL

How does this week's reading CALL to me? How am I being awakened with a greater sense of purpose and spirituality? How am I inspired to be a force for good in the world?

Day 4

CHALLENGE

How does this week's reading CHALLENGE me to grow? What am I now ready to adjust, release, forgive, and accept as a result of this week's reading?

WEEK

26

Day 5

CLARITY

What new CLARITY have I gained as a result of this week's reading? What better understanding do I now possess?

Day 6

COMFORT

What brings me COMFORT about this week's reading? How am I more at ease or consoled by this week's reading?

Day 7

CHANGE

How am I CHANGED by this week's reading? What insights, transforming thoughts, inner realizations, overcomings and breakthroughs am I now experiencing?

"I think everyone makes a mistake at least once in their life,
the important thing is what you learn from it..."
—Malala Yousafzai

Obedience

I follow the loving, guiding presence of God within me, and I complete what is mine to do.

> ***"Studying the Bible is more important than obeying it because if you don't understand it rightly you will obey it wrongly and your obedience will be disobedience."***
>
> **— Eugene H. Peterson**

What do you think of when you hear the word obedience? Does it trigger thoughts of submission, or generate feelings of defiance? Does it bring up issues around authority, and demands for compliance?

Society often views obedience as conformity and servility to an overbearing authority, or an act of weakness from an indebted and destitute soul. But can obedience mean something different? Can we display obedience without surrendering our dignity?

Spiritually speaking, obedience can have a softer, more loving connotation. Obedience to God is a natural occurrence to those who experience God's loving presence, and wants to remain in its blessed alignment. The need for willful resistance dissolves into a willingness to trust that all things truly are being beautifully orchestrated for the good of all concerned. In the midst of many appearances to the contrary, this not only requires a willingness, but also a discipline and a faith that is anything but weak.

The outcome of spiritual obedience is one of absolute abundance, and inexplicable joy, for the love of God is eternally seeking to bless you as you listen, then dutifully complete what is yours to do.

Obedience

REFLECTION QUESTION

In what ways have you
benefited when you obeyed your *First Mind*?

WEEK 27

Obedience

I follow the loving, guiding presence of God within me, and I complete what is mine to do.

Day 2

CENTER

How does this week's reading CENTER me and bring calm, balance, and breathing space to my worldview?

Day 3

CALL

How does this week's reading CALL to me? How am I being awakened with a greater sense of purpose and spirituality? How am I inspired to be a force for good in the world?

Day 4

CHALLENGE

How does this week's reading CHALLENGE me to grow? What am I now ready to adjust, release, forgive, and accept as a result of this week's reading?

WEEK

27

Day 5 **CLARITY**

What new CLARITY have I gained as a result of this week's reading? What better understanding do I now possess?

Day 6 **COMFORT**

What brings me COMFORT about this week's reading? How am I more at ease or consoled by this week's reading?

Day 7 **CHANGE**

How am I CHANGED by this week's reading? What insights, transforming thoughts, inner realizations, overcomings and breakthroughs am I now experiencing?

My life is weaved together as an orderly tapestry of Divine design.

"All things work together for the good of them who love the Lord and are called according to His purpose"
— Romans 8:28

When from among the busyness of our days we emerge long enough to pause, we can elect to switch positions from the participant in our lives to the observer of Life itself. And from this elevated space, we are in position to see that life is sequential. One thing builds on the next. One moment connects to the next. One hour gives rise to the next and the sunset on even the most challenging of days triggers the sunrise of the next.

Our lives are threaded by a single core of order and when we choose to align, rather than resist the orderly persistence that governs all of creation, we can clearly see the influence of Spirit in all of our affairs. When we live in resistance to this orderly flow, we activate the con-sequences that follow our disorderly conduct and our perception of the beauty, the harmony, the symmetry and the peace is clouded. Today, choose to fall back into the full awareness that there is a conspiracy of good meticulously orchestrated and organized on your behalf and witness peace rising in your life, world and in all of your affairs, like never before.

Order

REFLECTION QUESTION

What mysteries might be made clear to you when you allow yourself to recognize how order is established in your life?

WEEK 28

Order

My life is weaved together as an orderly tapestry of Divine design.

Day 2

CENTER

How does this week's reading CENTER me and bring calm, balance, and breathing space to my worldview?

Day 3

CALL

How does this week's reading CALL to me? How am I being awakened with a greater sense of purpose and spirituality? How am I inspired to be a force for good in the world?

Day 4

CHALLENGE

How does this week's reading CHALLENGE me to grow? What am I now ready to adjust, release, forgive, and accept as a result of this week's reading?

WEEK

28

Day 5

CLARITY

What new CLARITY have I gained as a result of this week's reading? What better understanding do I now possess?

Day 6

COMFORT

What brings me COMFORT about this week's reading? How am I more at ease or consoled by this week's reading?

Day 7

CHANGE

How am I CHANGED by this week's reading? What insights, transforming thoughts, inner realizations, overcomings and breakthroughs am I now experiencing?

I AM wiser because I use the information pain brings me to adjust.

"The School of Hard Knocks is among life's most effective, and yet unnecessary, institutions."

— Kevin Kitrell Ross

Despite the many ways it enters into our lives, the experience of pain in the Earth school is virtually inevitable. On its surface, pain is an unpleasant, disruptive experience that produces great discomfort, agony, and sometimes suffering. If this is the only experience that one is having of pain, then she may never fully grasp its benefits.

Pain can also be interpreted as information that is presented through the Earth School that notifies us of a significant adjustment that needs to be made. For instance, the pain one experiences as a result of someone's boot heel crushing their big toe, is information. The person whose toe is being injured must make an immediate adjustment from beneath the boot heel in order to prevent further harm. And while the person who is the wearer of the boot is the offender, waiting for the boot wearer to free one's big toe is the equivalent to giving him a pain reliever and hoping your toe will feel better as a result. We heal ourselves by making the necessary adjustments with the information we are given, even by Life's most painful experiences. In so doing, pain is a professor whose instruction carries the potential to make us wise.

Pain

REFLECTION QUESTION

What adjustments are being called
for by the painful experiences in your life?

WEEK 29

I AM wiser because I use the information pain brings me to adjust.

Day 2

CENTER

How does this week's reading CENTER me and bring calm, balance, and breathing space to my worldview?

Day 3

CALL

How does this week's reading CALL to me? How am I being awakened with a greater sense of purpose and spirituality? How am I inspired to be a force for good in the world?

Day 4

CHALLENGE

How does this week's reading CHALLENGE me to grow? What am I now ready to adjust, release, forgive, and accept as a result of this week's reading?

WEEK

29

Day 5 **CLARITY**

What new CLARITY have I gained as a result of this week's reading? What better understanding do I now possess?

Day 6 **COMFORT**

What brings me COMFORT about this week's reading? How am I more at ease or consoled by this week's reading?

Day 7 **CHANGE**

How am I CHANGED by this week's reading? What insights, transforming thoughts, inner realizations, overcomings and breakthroughs am I now experiencing?

Parenting

I AM fully equipped to handle all my affairs from the wisest place within me.

***"And when I became fully grown,
I put away childish things."***

— 1 Corinthians 13:11

Most everyone can find one admirable quality about their parents worth celebrating. Likewise, most everyone can find something for which to complain and lay blame upon their parents. In fact, most of the suffering in the human condition is attributed to being under-parented or over-parented. And it is upon these memories that we often choose to erect monuments of pain that block our momentum and the full development of our potential.

Today choose to liberate yourself of the false arrest of your own development by limiting your potential to the shortcomings of your parents. Stop. Take a breath and forgive them for doing too little or for doing too much. Forgive yourself for seeking to compete with those whose parenting was just right. Now, see all the years and all the lessons learned being embodied as wisdom in you. Trust that you are now and forever tapped into the pipeline of Omniscience and know that this is your guidance, your safe place, your healer and the lover and keeper of your soul.

Parenting

REFLECTION QUESTION

What untapped and untold joy
would be released into your life if you forgave your parents
for their shortcomings and forgave yourself for feeling
unworthy of the best?

WEEK 30

Parenting

I AM fully equipped to handle all my affairs from the wisest place within me.

Day 2

CENTER

How does this week's reading CENTER me and bring calm, balance, and breathing space to my worldview?

Day 3

CALL

How does this week's reading CALL to me? How am I being awakened with a greater sense of purpose and spirituality? How am I inspired to be a force for good in the world?

Day 4

CHALLENGE

How does this week's reading CHALLENGE me to grow? What am I now ready to adjust, release, forgive, and accept as a result of this week's reading?

WEEK

30

Day 5

CLARITY

What new CLARITY have I gained as a result of this week's reading? What better understanding do I now possess?

Day 6

COMFORT

What brings me COMFORT about this week's reading? How am I more at ease or consoled by this week's reading?

Day 7

CHANGE

How am I CHANGED by this week's reading? What insights, transforming thoughts, inner realizations, overcomings and breakthroughs am I now experiencing?

"Admitting the weighty problems and staggering disappointments, . . .God is able to give us the power to meet them. [God] is able to give us the inner equilibrium to stand tall amid the trials and burdens of life. . . [and] is able to provide inner peace amid outer storms."

—Martin Luther King, Jr.

I make a declaration of peace by being true to myself first.

"Those who make peaceful revolution impossible will make violent revolution inevitable."

— John F. Kennedy

I grew up hearing and singing a song which wonderfully proclaimed, *"Let there be peace on earth and let it begin with me."* As I sang the song, images of a war-free planet, overflowing with understanding people filled my mind. As I have grown and matured, the song's meaning has deepened. Peace has become more than the absence of war; as if war is the opposite of peace. In actuality, peace is the resolution of any disturbance or disturbing thought, especially those inhabiting my own soul.

What is paradoxically perplexing about peace in this context, is that addressing these disturbances may require a confrontation. This is why peace by no means is silent. The confrontation does not have to be hostile or violent. It can be candid and forthright. Whether it's speaking truth to power, being honest with myself, or standing up for what's right, such encounters can result in a soulful tranquility, in the knowledge that such inner turmoil has no place to hide and has been dealt with.

It is in that moment, I find myself at peace, and my soul is serene and at ease.

Peace

REFLECTION QUESTION

What unresolved issues do you have
an opportunity to address through a personal treaty of peace
that can bring tranquility and order to your life?

WEEK 31

I make a declaration of peace by being true to myself first.

Day 2 **CENTER**

How does this week's reading CENTER me and bring calm, balance, and breathing space to my worldview?

Day 3 **CALL**

How does this week's reading CALL to me? How am I being awakened with a greater sense of purpose and spirituality? How am I inspired to be a force for good in the world?

Day 4 **CHALLENGE**

How does this week's reading CHALLENGE me to grow? What am I now ready to adjust, release, forgive, and accept as a result of this week's reading?

WEEK

31

Day 5 **CLARITY**

What new CLARITY have I gained as a result of this week's reading? What better understanding do I now possess?

Day 6 **COMFORT**

What brings me COMFORT about this week's reading? How am I more at ease or consoled by this week's reading?

Day 7 **CHANGE**

How am I CHANGED by this week's reading? What insights, transforming thoughts, inner realizations, overcomings and breakthroughs am I now experiencing?

I pray, therefore, I AM.

"Your Father knows what you have need of before you ask..."

— Matthew 6:8

More and more we are hearing those disturbed by the various injustices and violent outbursts lift their voices in protest toward those who have been given the power to effect change. In fact, this is occurring at such an alarming rate, that when politicians and others in authority offer their "thoughts, prayers and condolences" for those affected by these atrocities, their words have begun to ring hollow. People are seeking action, and want change so deeply, that the effectiveness of such "prayers" are in question. "Enough prayer," is the cry. "Action" is the call.

But what is prayer if not a petition? True prayer has always been an effective agency for change. In prayer we pause when we find ourselves in a constant outcry for change; protesting when the life of our collective making does not meet our desires or expectations. It is then, often in desperate objection, that we present ourselves before Spirit as living petitions for the life we wish to live, and for what we'd like to see and to be.

Perhaps rather than pushing prayer aside, we should seek to embody the petitions we offer within them. Protest indeed has its place in communicating what we would like to change, but eventually we must effectively fill our thoughts, our minds, our hearts, and the void with a vision and manifestation of what that change can be. With God, our petitions become charged with Divine energy and power, and as we continue to pray, we discover we have all the help we need. Through our prayerful petitions, we become the change we'd like to see.

Petition

REFLECTION QUESTION

What prayers can only be
answered through your embodied petition?

WEEK 32

I pray, therefore, I AM.

Day 2

CENTER

How does this week's reading CENTER me and bring calm, balance, and breathing space to my worldview?

Day 3

CALL

How does this week's reading CALL to me? How am I being awakened with a greater sense of purpose and spirituality? How am I inspired to be a force for good in the world?

Day 4

CHALLENGE

How does this week's reading CHALLENGE me to grow? What am I now ready to adjust, release, forgive, and accept as a result of this week's reading?

Day 5 CLARITY

What new CLARITY have I gained as a result of this week's reading? What better understanding do I now possess?

Day 6 COMFORT

What brings me COMFORT about this week's reading? How am I more at ease or consoled by this week's reading?

Day 7 CHANGE

How am I CHANGED by this week's reading? What insights, transforming thoughts, inner realizations, overcomings and breakthroughs am I now experiencing?

I am a perpetual fount of the gifts of Spirit.

"A person's relationship to poverty or prosperity can be determined in the positioning of his cup. When he turns his cup upward he is a candidate to receive. When he turns his cup downward, he loses what he has in his cup and nothing more can get in. I travel with my cup and my saucer firmly affixed under the bottom of my cup because I understand God's only measure is overflow."

— Kevin Kitrell Ross

For every soul there comes a breaking point. That is, a breaking through the limitations of the immature, underdeveloped stage of spiritual adolescence into the fully matured, fully developed life of devoted service. It is at this exact intersection in the unfolding of one's soul that he experiences what it means to be "poured out." Being "poured out" is to being granted full access to the power to fulfill your dreams. It is to be in the perpetual receipt, acceptance, development and delivery of the assignment that has been given to your life.

This is when each soul meets its most prolific self. Like Alexander Hamilton, who's great passion for the New World, fused with his gift for writing and his pouring out produced for our nation, The Federalist Papers — that which would eventually be the foundation for the Constitution of the United States of America. Like Hamilton, when our souls have peered through the preoccupation with the solvable sins of the small self and yields to the seismic seduction of the Greater Self, then the fun truly beings. We get to witness how creative we can be, how strong we can be, how disciplined we can be, how generous we can be, how determined we can be, how versatile we can be and indeed, how rich and prosperous we can be. It is in being poured out that I learn to trust the Hand that is doing the pouring and love the soul that is overflowing.

Pour

REFLECTION QUESTION

What would it be like for you
to experience your life overflowing with every kind of good?

WEEK 33

I am a perpetual fount of the gifts of Spirit.

Day 2 **CENTER**

How does this week's reading CENTER me and bring calm, balance, and breathing space to my worldview?

Day 3 **CALL**

How does this week's reading CALL to me? How am I being awakened with a greater sense of purpose and spirituality? How am I inspired to be a force for good in the world?

Day 4 **CHALLENGE**

How does this week's reading CHALLENGE me to grow? What am I now ready to adjust, release, forgive, and accept as a result of this week's reading?

WEEK

33

Day 5 **CLARITY**

What new CLARITY have I gained as a result of this week's reading? What better understanding do I now possess?

Day 6 **COMFORT**

What brings me COMFORT about this week's reading? How am I more at ease or consoled by this week's reading?

Day 7 **CHANGE**

How am I CHANGED by this week's reading? What insights, transforming thoughts, inner realizations, overcomings and breakthroughs am I now experiencing?

Questions

The answer to every question I ask reveals another aspect of me.

"True religion is . . . an invitation into a journey that leads one toward the mystery of God. Idolatry is religion pretending that it has all the answers."

—John Shelby Spong

Who am I? Why did this happen to me? What happens next? How do I overcome? Where do I go from here? When will I win?" These are some of the deep questions swirling in the dark, unanswered desires of our hearts. Such questions often lead us directly into the entryway of a daunting and infinite unknown. Answers to the mysteries of life is part of an eternal and marvelous mystique we experience in God. Our lives intertwine with this mystery as our actions create consequences, and each consequence is an answer that can lead to more questions! Each mystery that is revealed can also be a doorway to deeper mysteries, and while there are answers to them all, it may not be our time to know.

But be encouraged beloved, for there is a quest operating in the question; an intriguing journey we are being summoned to take. On this journey, we learn about ourselves as much as we discover the answer to our questions. In this light, the answer to every question is you.

Ask the question. Embrace the mystery. Take the journey. Enjoy the answer.

Questions

REFLECTION QUESTION

What questions, were you to
ask them, would reveal a new truth about you?

Questions

The answer to every question I ask reveals another aspect of me.

Day 2

CENTER

How does this week's reading CENTER me and bring calm, balance, and breathing space to my worldview?

Day 3

CALL

How does this week's reading CALL to me? How am I being awakened with a greater sense of purpose and spirituality? How am I inspired to be a force for good in the world?

Day 4

CHALLENGE

How does this week's reading CHALLENGE me to grow? What am I now ready to adjust, release, forgive, and accept as a result of this week's reading?

WEEK

34

Day 5 **CLARITY**

What new CLARITY have I gained as a result of this week's reading? What better understanding do I now possess?

____

____

____

____

Day 6 **COMFORT**

What brings me COMFORT about this week's reading? How am I more at ease or consoled by this week's reading?

____

____

____

____

Day 7 **CHANGE**

How am I CHANGED by this week's reading? What insights, transforming thoughts, inner realizations, overcomings and breakthroughs am I now experiencing?

____

____

____

____

Quickening

I am open and receptive to the constant quickening of the Spirit.

"There is a vitality, a life force, an energy, a quickening, that is translated through you into action, and because there is only one of you in all time, this expression is unique."

— Martha Graham

It is reassuring that the Omnipresence of Spirit is ever available to revive, recharge and restore our minds, our hearts and our bodies. Whenever we are inundated with worry, or paralyzed with fear; whenever we are baffled or confused, in a fog or lose our way; when we feel down and depressed, or tired and out of breath, we can readily connect and be spiritually quickened through prayer and meditation.

Spiritual quickening is an infusion of Divine energy emerging within your being. It can feel like a second wind, or a breath of fresh air, yet does more than fill your lungs or freshen the room. It invigorates the mind. It restores the soul. It enlivens whatever it touches. It awakens the body. It stimulates the senses. It clarifies and verifies. It mends and heals, and does so all at once for those who are receptive to the realization.

Find a quiet place to rest your mind and your heart of life's current appearances. For the moment, let go of your worries and fears. Sit your questions aside. Place what you are searching for on pause. Lay your judgments down. Take deep cleansing breaths and repeatedly speak the following words:

"I call on the help of the Holy Spirit. I realize that the Spirit of God is the spirit in me, and I am open and receptive to Its constant and complete quickening. I allow this quickening to restore my mind, soul, my body, my life, my heart, my health, my outlook, my in-look, my work, my finances and my affairs."

REFLECTION QUESTION

What other areas in
your life could use a spiritual quickening?

WEEK 35

I am open and receptive to the constant quickening of the Spirit.

Day 2

CENTER

How does this week's reading CENTER me and bring calm, balance, and breathing space to my worldview?

Day 3

CALL

How does this week's reading CALL to me? How am I being awakened with a greater sense of purpose and spirituality? How am I inspired to be a force for good in the world?

Day 4

CHALLENGE

How does this week's reading CHALLENGE me to grow? What am I now ready to adjust, release, forgive, and accept as a result of this week's reading?

WEEK

35

Day 5 **CLARITY**

What new CLARITY have I gained as a result of this week's reading? What better understanding do I now possess?

Day 6 **COMFORT**

What brings me COMFORT about this week's reading? How am I more at ease or consoled by this week's reading?

Day 7 **CHANGE**

How am I CHANGED by this week's reading? What insights, transforming thoughts, inner realizations, overcomings and breakthroughs am I now experiencing?

> *"We cannot seek achievement for ourselves and forget about progress and prosperity for our community… Our ambitions must be broad enough to include the aspirations and needs of others, for their sakes and for our own."*
>
> —Cesar Chavez

I shine with purpose, and my life is my message.

"You are the light of the world..."

— Matthew 5:14

In many pictures, Jesus and other ascended sages are painted with halos and auras around their faces, hands and bodies. It is to depict that the person has special character, and has come to do something significant on the earth.

An aura is a certain emanating light or glow that others can see around another. It reflects the energy a person carries. It telegraphs the message held in one's heart, and it is an indicator of one's purpose on the planet.

The Life force that generates auras radiates from everyone. We see it in mothers that are pregnant with a child, and newborns themselves. We see it in lovers, both new and with many years together. We see it in celebrities with unique talents, and leaders of many nations. Our auras become more apparent as we share what we have come to contribute in the world. Auras are spiritual medals; a universal recognition from all who see you shine.

Radiate!

REFLECTION QUESTION

Whose aura do you
recognize that shines brightly in your life?

I shine with purpose, and my life is my message.

Day 2 **CENTER**

How does this week's reading CENTER me and bring calm, balance, and breathing space to my worldview?

Day 3 **CALL**

How does this week's reading CALL to me? How am I being awakened with a greater sense of purpose and spirituality? How am I inspired to be a force for good in the world?

Day 4 **CHALLENGE**

How does this week's reading CHALLENGE me to grow? What am I now ready to adjust, release, forgive, and accept as a result of this week's reading?

WEEK
36

Day 5 **CLARITY**

What new CLARITY have I gained as a result of this week's reading? What better understanding do I now possess?

Day 6 **COMFORT**

What brings me COMFORT about this week's reading? How am I more at ease or consoled by this week's reading?

Day 7 **CHANGE**

How am I CHANGED by this week's reading? What insights, transforming thoughts, inner realizations, overcomings and breakthroughs am I now experiencing?

Scatter

My ideas produce in due season when I nurture them.

"It's not what you gather, but what you scatter that tells what kind of life you lived."

— Helen Walton

The quality and the quantity of what is harvested in life is determined by the seeds sown, the soil the seeds are planted in, and the season!

What is gathered in any harvest is first determined by what is scattered. Seeds are like ideas that are seeking to sprout into a corresponding produce, but they must be planted in fertile and nurturing soil. Finally, the soil is constantly conditioned by the season, which sets the environment for growth.

Seek seed ideas for anything you desire to harvest in life. Plant yourself in spaces that are welcoming and receptive to those ideas. In due season, the fruit of your labor will appear.

Scatter

REFLECTION QUESTION

Has the time come for me
to act on any ideas lying dormant in my mind?

WEEK

37

Scatter

My ideas produce in due season when I nurture them.

Day 2

CENTER

How does this week's reading CENTER me and bring calm, balance, and breathing space to my worldview?

Day 3

CALL

How does this week's reading CALL to me? How am I being awakened with a greater sense of purpose and spirituality? How am I inspired to be a force for good in the world?

Day 4

CHALLENGE

How does this week's reading CHALLENGE me to grow? What am I now ready to adjust, release, forgive, and accept as a result of this week's reading?

WEEK

37

Day 5 **CLARITY**

What new CLARITY have I gained as a result of this week's reading? What better understanding do I now possess?

Day 6 **COMFORT**

What brings me COMFORT about this week's reading? How am I more at ease or consoled by this week's reading?

Day 7 **CHANGE**

How am I CHANGED by this week's reading? What insights, transforming thoughts, inner realizations, overcomings and breakthroughs am I now experiencing?

Scream

I use the power of my voice to release stress, break tension, and relieve frustration!

""Shout, shout. Let it all out. These are the things I can do without. Come on. I'm talking to you. Come on."

— Lyrics to "Tears for Fears"
by Orzabal Roland and Stanley Ian

Anxiety. Stress. Frustration. Deadlines. Setbacks. Disappointments. We all have them. The question is, "Are they having us?" What are we doing with the ordinary pressures that come with the territory of life as an adult? Have we found proactive ways of managing these pressures or are we allowing the pressures to cause us to act out of character? Before you lose your temper, flip your top, slam the door, or spin out of control—SCREAM! Yes, you read correctly. SCREAM!

Like a teapot or a steam engine that's reached a boiling point, the pressure that builds inside can be harnessed for some productive outcome. As conscious beings, we can choose to relieve ourselves intentionally of the built up pressures of life by having a double-lunged, full-voiced scream. It's a scream, not aimed at someone, but a scream made for someone—you. Consider it a mental health scream. Scream in a pillow. Scream in an open field. Scream in a closet. Scream in an empty room. Scream in the basement. Scream in the garage. But, by all means—get it out! Transmute that nagging stress into roaring liberation with an intentional scream.

Scream

REFLECTION QUESTION

What pressures do you accumulate
that could qualify you as a candidate for a big scream?

WEEK
38

Scream

I use the power of my voice to release stress, break tension, and relieve frustration!

Day 2

CENTER

How does this week's reading CENTER me and bring calm, balance, and breathing space to my worldview?

Day 3

CALL

How does this week's reading CALL to me? How am I being awakened with a greater sense of purpose and spirituality? How am I inspired to be a force for good in the world?

Day 4

CHALLENGE

How does this week's reading CHALLENGE me to grow? What am I now ready to adjust, release, forgive, and accept as a result of this week's reading?

WEEK

38

Day 5 **CLARITY**

What new CLARITY have I gained as a result of this week's reading? What better understanding do I now possess?

Day 6 **COMFORT**

What brings me COMFORT about this week's reading? How am I more at ease or consoled by this week's reading?

Day 7 **CHANGE**

How am I CHANGED by this week's reading? What insights, transforming thoughts, inner realizations, overcomings and breakthroughs am I now experiencing?

I move with confidence in my every pursuit, for all that I need to know is revealed in Divine Order.

"Search and you will find."

— Matthew 7:7

Most people have experienced having that sinking feeling in the pit of their stomachs when they discover they've somehow lost something precious to them. That initial panic can be paralyzing. It makes us feel vulnerable, helpless, and sometimes angry with ourselves. The lost keys, misplaced wallet, child that gets separated from us in a department store, an important document, or a missing cell phone are all outward manifestations of a momentary lapse of a conscious connection to the present moment. Settle your sense of anxiety, by shutting out your obsessive focus on the outer absence of the missing thing, and with a deep conscious breath, turn within and connect to that field of Omnipresence and Omniscience. For just there in the spaces between inhale and exhale is the access point to the Mind of Spirit, which sees all, knows all, is orchestrating all things to work together for your good. Search there and you will find.

Search

REFLECTION QUESTION

What possible benefit is it
to you when you lose something you treasure?

WEEK 39

Search

I move with confidence in my every pursuit, for all that I need to know is revealed in Divine Order.

Day 2

CENTER

How does this week's reading CENTER me and bring calm, balance, and breathing space to my worldview?

Day 3

CALL

How does this week's reading CALL to me? How am I being awakened with a greater sense of purpose and spirituality? How am I inspired to be a force for good in the world?

Day 4

CHALLENGE

How does this week's reading CHALLENGE me to grow? What am I now ready to adjust, release, forgive, and accept as a result of this week's reading?

WEEK

39

Day 5 **CLARITY**

What new CLARITY have I gained as a result of this week's reading? What better understanding do I now possess?

Day 6 **COMFORT**

What brings me COMFORT about this week's reading? How am I more at ease or consoled by this week's reading?

Day 7 **CHANGE**

How am I CHANGED by this week's reading? What insights, transforming thoughts, inner realizations, overcomings and breakthroughs am I now experiencing?

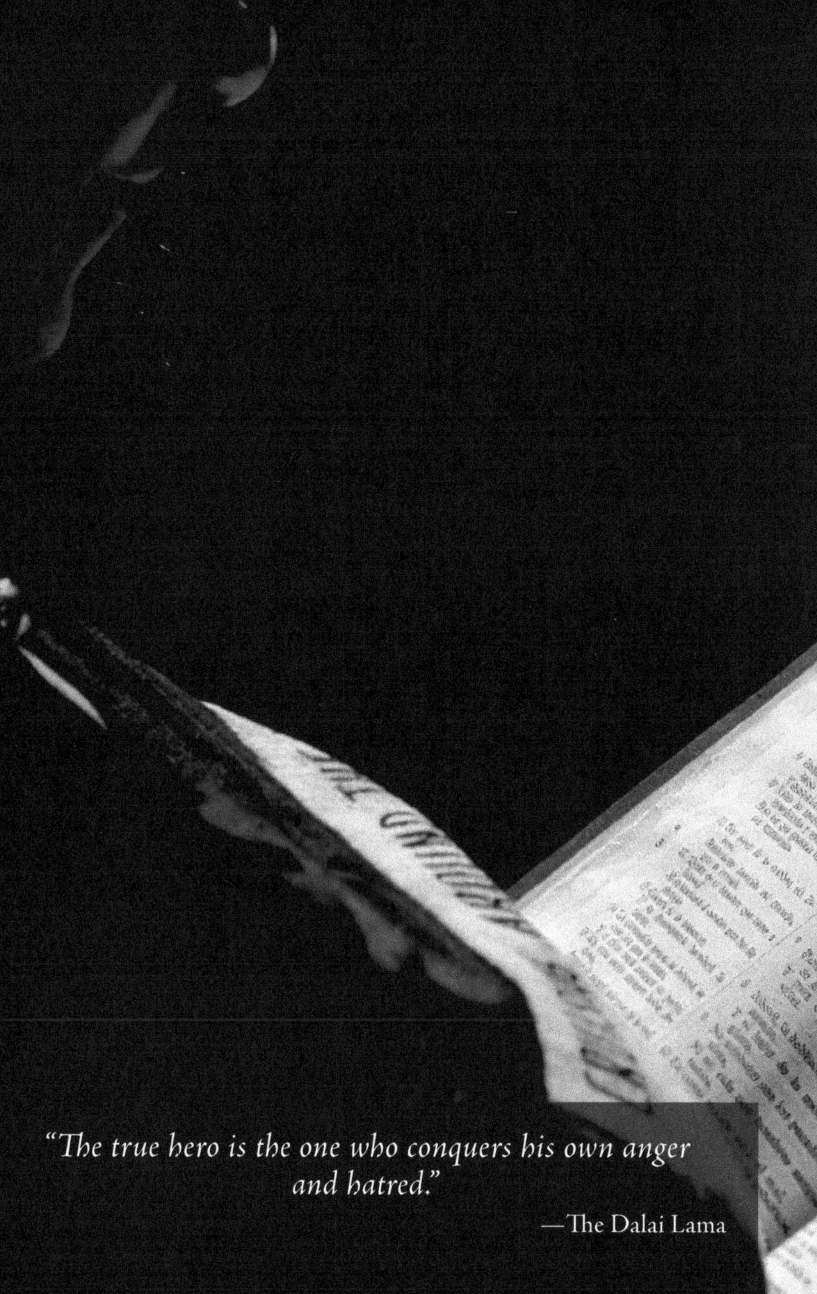

“The true hero is the one who conquers his own anger and hatred.”

—The Dalai Lama

Seasons

I am changing for the better and I embrace better approaches to change. I am always open to better ways and a better me.

"He who rejects change is the architect of decay. The only human institution which rejects progress is the cemetery."
— Harold Wilson

It has been said that the only thing in life that is certain is that life will change. Humorously however, the uncertainty of change (and the certainty of what is) often has us resisting change, and desperately holding on to things we should have released long ago. People struggle to hold onto our youthful appearance, completely rejecting the beauty of their emerging maturity. Generations resist new and improved advancements, not because there is skepticism about its efficacy, but because they have become accustomed to what they have come to know.

Certainly, change—even if it is for the better—can be inconvenient, and can challenge who we assume ourselves to be. Yet there are ways to embrace change without fear, and do so with far less struggle. First, take a deep breath, and receive from a space of Oneness with Infinite Knowingness the guidance that Solomon in his wisdom came to accept and realize; that all things have a season. Seasons are the containers of change, and can allow us to move fluidly from one change to the next. There is a time for every purpose under the heavens, therefore, align yourself with the season, be it a season of sowing the seeds of new ideas, or a season of nurture, blossom and growth. We can work within seasons of fruitfulness, harvest and enjoyment. We can also work within seasons of release, retooling and preparation for the good that is next. Seasons can help us be aware of the time; the time to stay present and vigilant, the time to reflect and honor lessons of the past, and the time for change and to be ever hopeful for all that the future holds.

Thank you Beneficent Spirit, for seasons of change that bring opportunities for improvement and positive outcomes for all.

Seasons

REFLECTION QUESTION

If you were assured of a positive or improved outcome, what things in your life would you be willing to change?

WEEK 40

Seasons

I am changing for the better and I embrace better approaches to change. I am always open to better ways and a better me.

Day 2 **CENTER**

How does this week's reading CENTER me and bring calm, balance, and breathing space to my worldview?

Day 3 **CALL**

How does this week's reading CALL to me? How am I being awakened with a greater sense of purpose and spirituality? How am I inspired to be a force for good in the world?

Day 4 **CHALLENGE**

How does this week's reading CHALLENGE me to grow? What am I now ready to adjust, release, forgive, and accept as a result of this week's reading?

WEEK

40

Day 5 CLARITY

What new CLARITY have I gained as a result of this week's reading? What better understanding do I now possess?

Day 6 COMFORT

What brings me COMFORT about this week's reading? How am I more at ease or consoled by this week's reading?

Day 7 CHANGE

How am I CHANGED by this week's reading? What insights, transforming thoughts, inner realizations, overcomings and breakthroughs am I now experiencing?

I remain poised and centered amidst life's most turbulent storms.

"Lest our feet stray from the places our God where we met thee. Lest our hearts, drunk with the wine of the world we forget thee"

— James Weldon Johnson

Thinking is our ability to weigh concepts and ideas for ourselves in order to determine the best possibility and path for their application in our lives. When a person is impaired from the ability to think clearly, it is likely that he has become intoxicated by a strong emotion like anger, or entangled in the quicksand of depression, or overconfident by the hyper-reliance upon ego, or stuck by an absolute adherence to an extreme political or religious conviction. He may also simply be in bondage to an addiction to substances like alcohol or drugs.

Having sobriety is having ownership of your best and most essential self. It is being in full possession of your breath and living with the capacity to auto-regulate. Having sobriety is having a firm grip around what makes you-you and what makes for the living of a sound, centered, Spirit-led life. Living in sobriety allows us to detect the overuse or underuse of anything or anyone that could impair us from directing and enjoying our energies in meaningful and rewarding ways.

REFLECTION QUESTION

How far from sober have you ventured and how do you find your way back home?

WEEK 41

I remain poised and centered amidst life's most turbulent storms.

Day 2

CENTER

How does this week's reading CENTER me and bring calm, balance, and breathing space to my worldview?

Day 3

CALL

How does this week's reading CALL to me? How am I being awakened with a greater sense of purpose and spirituality? How am I inspired to be a force for good in the world?

Day 4

CHALLENGE

How does this week's reading CHALLENGE me to grow? What am I now ready to adjust, release, forgive, and accept as a result of this week's reading?

WEEK

41

Day 5 **CLARITY**

What new CLARITY have I gained as a result of this week's reading? What better understanding do I now possess?

Day 6 **COMFORT**

What brings me COMFORT about this week's reading? How am I more at ease or consoled by this week's reading?

Day 7 **CHANGE**

How am I CHANGED by this week's reading? What insights, transforming thoughts, inner realizations, overcomings and breakthroughs am I now experiencing?

Solace

I am lifted out of doldrums when I take solace, and it gives me great comfort and consolation.

"When the dog bites, When the bee stings, When I'm feeling sad; I simply remember my favorite things, And then I don't feel so bad."

— Lyrics from the song, Favorite Things

Recently I watched a news story about forest fires quickly spreading in California. I saw a group of firefighters lying motionless on the ground, covered in soot, attempting to gather themselves from spending a full day grappling to gain control of the fires. In this dark and gloomy moment, the firefighters suddenly began to sing. It became clear that although they were exhausted, they would soon be ready to continue to fight the blaze until it was contained.

Not everything in life works the way we expect. Sometimes our plans go up in smoke. Other times it seems as though we are fighting a losing battle and feelings of disappointment, stress and dismay set in. In moments like these it is good to know we can take solace.

Solace is what one looks to for comfort in times of distress or sadness. It is that person, place, thing or practice that helps us get past the stagnation and reconnect to the good that is our true reality. Solace takes our minds off of our difficulties. Solace centers. Solace consoles. Solace relieves and Solace soothes.

There is no need to wait for a problem to arise to discover what brings you solace. Many activities can bring solace to disappointing situations. Dive into a book. Dig into the dirt. Jot in a journal. Sink into a musical selection. Sing a song. Call a 3 AM friend.

However it happens, solace, when taken, clears up any mental fogginess or debris that may keep us from seeing the good that's ahead of us, if we just keep our heads up.

Solace

REFLECTION QUESTION

What people, places, things
and practices could you list that provides solace for you in
a dismal situation?

WEEK 42

Solace

I am lifted out of doldrums when I take solace, and it gives me great comfort and consolation.

Day 2

CENTER

How does this week's reading CENTER me and bring calm, balance, and breathing space to my worldview?

Day 3

CALL

How does this week's reading CALL to me? How am I being awakened with a greater sense of purpose and spirituality? How am I inspired to be a force for good in the world?

Day 4

CHALLENGE

How does this week's reading CHALLENGE me to grow? What am I now ready to adjust, release, forgive, and accept as a result of this week's reading?

WEEK

42

Day 5 **CLARITY**

What new CLARITY have I gained as a result of this week's reading? What better understanding do I now possess?

Day 6 **COMFORT**

What brings me COMFORT about this week's reading? How am I more at ease or consoled by this week's reading?

Day 7 **CHANGE**

How am I CHANGED by this week's reading? What insights, transforming thoughts, inner realizations, overcomings and breakthroughs am I now experiencing?

All I need to know comes to me easily, effortlessly and freely.

"You cannot even get your next breath, until you give away the one you have."

— Rev. Ike

Struggling is a common human experience. It is driven by a strong will and burning desire to be, to do, or to have something. It is the hopeful pushing against a mental, physical , or spiritual barrier in exchange for the elusive reward that initiated the struggle.

What we are to remember is that we are rewarded in the subtle spaces between effort and non-effort. The author is relieved of his writer's block, not while struggling for the next sentence, but in giving way to his mental fatigue. Stepping back is not quitting, it is the non-physical action required to give the Universe its cue, so that invisible, inaudible, and intangible choreography may be activated on your behalf. It is when the surface mind is at rest that it is free to see clearly, the path forward.

Step Back

REFLECTION QUESTION

What struggles do you need to step back from in order to discover the clear path to your freedom?

WEEK 43

All I need to know comes to me easily, effortlessly and freely.

Day 2

CENTER

How does this week's reading CENTER me and bring calm, balance, and breathing space to my worldview?

Day 3

CALL

How does this week's reading CALL to me? How am I being awakened with a greater sense of purpose and spirituality? How am I inspired to be a force for good in the world?

Day 4

CHALLENGE

How does this week's reading CHALLENGE me to grow? What am I now ready to adjust, release, forgive, and accept as a result of this week's reading?

WEEK

43

Day 5 **CLARITY**

What new CLARITY have I gained as a result of this week's reading? What better understanding do I now possess?

Day 6 **COMFORT**

What brings me COMFORT about this week's reading? How am I more at ease or consoled by this week's reading?

Day 7 **CHANGE**

How am I CHANGED by this week's reading? What insights, transforming thoughts, inner realizations, overcomings and breakthroughs am I now experiencing?

Sweetness

I heighten my awareness to experience the sweetness of life.

"I believe it pisses God off if you walk by the color purple in a field somewhere and don't notice it."
— Alice Walker, The Color Purple

Among life's most treasured experiences is that of sweetness. It is the appeal to the inner self to behold beauty. Whether it be the beauty of a sunrise or the beauty in the giggle of a newborn's laughter or the beauty in the joy shared between two old friends or the beauty of a field of flowers adorned in purple, our deep inner attraction to beauty opens us to the experience of sweetness in ourselves and thereby we have the ability to sense, behold, and relish in the sweetness of others and in the world around us.

Sweetness is there to be slowly embraced, to be patiently savored, to be fondly remembered, and to eagerly pursue. Her address is in the eye of the beholder. Her memory is on the lips of the grateful.

Sweetness

REFLECTION QUESTION

What opportunities are there
for you to heighten your awareness to the experience of
everyday sweetness?

Sweetness

I heighten my awareness to experience the sweetness of life.

Day 2 **CENTER**

How does this week's reading CENTER me and bring calm, balance, and breathing space to my worldview?

____

____

____

____

Day 3 **CALL**

How does this week's reading CALL to me? How am I being awakened with a greater sense of purpose and spirituality? How am I inspired to be a force for good in the world?

____

____

____

____

Day 4 **CHALLENGE**

How does this week's reading CHALLENGE me to grow? What am I now ready to adjust, release, forgive, and accept as a result of this week's reading?

____

____

____

____

Day 5 CLARITY

What new CLARITY have I gained as a result of this week's reading? What better understanding do I now possess?

Day 6 COMFORT

What brings me COMFORT about this week's reading? How am I more at ease or consoled by this week's reading?

Day 7 CHANGE

How am I CHANGED by this week's reading? What insights, transforming thoughts, inner realizations, overcomings and breakthroughs am I now experiencing?

"If you bring forth what is within you, what you bring forth will save you. If you do not bring forth what is within you, what you do not bring forth will destroy you."

—Jesus, The Gospel of Thomas

I graciously and gratefully acknowledge and accept all the good God promptly and perpetually provides.

"I find myself giving thanks as unceasingly as I pray, for God has been just that reliable."

— Eric Ovid Donaldson

Parades and games, the reunion of family and friends, and the breaking of bread marks the day we celebrate as Thanksgiving. It is a national holiday in many countries, and is the appreciation of the manifestation or fruition of the good. On Thanksgiving day, we feast on what is filling and savory, as well as fulfilling and gratifying.

After a satisfying feast, many people often find a place to digest what has been gathered, prepared, presented and partaken. This is also an excellent opportunity to spiritually do the same.

Take time to find a quiet space where you can gratefully reflect on the good that has manifested for you this year. Take in and feast on the love with which each good that has blessed you. Acknowledge all who were involved in its fruition, its preparation, its presentation, and its enjoyment, and give thanks to God for filling your life with joy and gladness.

This simple exercise in thanksgiving connects, expands and extends the joy we feel unto others, and makes a day more memorable and meaningful for all.

Thanksgiving

REFLECTION QUESTION

If you were to sit down now with a pen and a pad of paper, how long a list could you create for all you are grateful for today alone?

WEEK 45

Thanksgiving

I graciously and gratefully acknowledge and accept all the good God promptly and perpetually provides.

Day 2

CENTER

How does this week's reading CENTER me and bring calm, balance, and breathing space to my worldview?

Day 3

CALL

How does this week's reading CALL to me? How am I being awakened with a greater sense of purpose and spirituality? How am I inspired to be a force for good in the world?

Day 4

CHALLENGE

How does this week's reading CHALLENGE me to grow? What am I now ready to adjust, release, forgive, and accept as a result of this week's reading?

WEEK

45

Day 5 **CLARITY**

What new CLARITY have I gained as a result of this week's reading? What better understanding do I now possess?

Day 6 **COMFORT**

What brings me COMFORT about this week's reading? How am I more at ease or consoled by this week's reading?

Day 7 **CHANGE**

How am I CHANGED by this week's reading? What insights, transforming thoughts, inner realizations, overcomings and breakthroughs am I now experiencing?

Understanding

As I grow more understanding, I am of greater service to humanity.

"And with all your getting, get understanding."
— Proverbs 4:7

Life is ever and always extending us the invitation to know more, to discover, to be dazzled and even baffled by its magnificent mysteries and wonders. As souls on assignment, the most healthy posture we can assume is that of openness, curiosity, and a willingness to learn. It is with this beginner's mind that we are candidates for insights, revelations, and that we deepen our understanding about the inner-workings of our own souls, the universe, and Life itself.

As we attain greater understanding about the mysteries that are hidden by our human blind spots, the territory of our compassion is enlarged, the well of our patience becomes bottomless and we become infertile territory to produce or reproduce hate in any of its forms.

With greater understanding, we become greater channels for healing, revealing, and building a more kind, just, global society.

Understanding

REFLECTION QUESTION

What blinds of misunderstanding need to be raised so that you can serve humanity with more compassion?

WEEK 46

Understanding

As I grow more understanding, I am of greater service to humanity.

Day 2

CENTER

How does this week's reading CENTER me and bring calm, balance, and breathing space to my worldview?

Day 3

CALL

How does this week's reading CALL to me? How am I being awakened with a greater sense of purpose and spirituality? How am I inspired to be a force for good in the world?

Day 4

CHALLENGE

How does this week's reading CHALLENGE me to grow? What am I now ready to adjust, release, forgive, and accept as a result of this week's reading?

WEEK

46

Day 5 **CLARITY**

What new CLARITY have I gained as a result of this week's reading? What better understanding do I now possess?

Day 6 **COMFORT**

What brings me COMFORT about this week's reading? How am I more at ease or consoled by this week's reading?

Day 7 **CHANGE**

How am I CHANGED by this week's reading? What insights, transforming thoughts, inner realizations, overcomings and breakthroughs am I now experiencing?

Voice

I channel my vision, my values and my views through the power of my voice!

"You shall decree a thing and it shall be established unto you and the light shall shine upon your ways."

— Job 22:8

Every soul that moves through the Earth school is a bright unfolding idea, sent to be a unique expression and extension of Spirit. Our individual journeys give us greater and greater insight into who we have "truly" come here to be. Our experiences, be they easy or difficult, lengthy or brief, random or significant, are shaping us and opening us to our most authentic selves. It is in coming to know, love and accept our authentic selves that our true voice emerges. The voice is more than the acoustic sound that emanates from speech.

Our voice is our fully unified and integrated self. It is an indivisible expression of who we are — free from contraction, falsehood, and fear. It can be found in our artistic expression, our activism, and our academic body of work. Our voice is our verbal signature on life's most important issues. When we find the voice of the genuine within us, we access the power to call the world we see, with our mind's eye, into visible manifestation.

REFLECTION QUESTION

When you use your voice,
what difference is made on the planet?

I channel my vision, my values and my views through the power of my voice!

Day 2 **CENTER**

How does this week's reading CENTER me and bring calm, balance, and breathing space to my worldview?

____

____

____

____

Day 3 **CALL**

How does this week's reading CALL to me? How am I being awakened with a greater sense of purpose and spirituality? How am I inspired to be a force for good in the world?

____

____

____

____

Day 4 **CHALLENGE**

How does this week's reading CHALLENGE me to grow? What am I now ready to adjust, release, forgive, and accept as a result of this week's reading?

____

____

____

____

WEEK

47

Day 5 **CLARITY**

What new CLARITY have I gained as a result of this week's reading? What better understanding do I now possess?

Day 6 **COMFORT**

What brings me COMFORT about this week's reading? How am I more at ease or consoled by this week's reading?

Day 7 **CHANGE**

How am I CHANGED by this week's reading? What insights, transforming thoughts, inner realizations, overcomings and breakthroughs am I now experiencing?

I seek to welcome others into my space with the dignity of an ambassador and the warmth of family.

"Actions anywhere, can have impact everywhere."
— Eric Ovid Donaldson

Society's wonderful technological advances have connected countries and cultures in ways unimaginable just a few decades ago. Technology used to catapult astronauts, satellites, and probes into the vast cosmos has now brought humankind closer through phones, tablets, and laptops; most with cameras and supported through social platforms. People with cultural differences—whether demarcated by border checkpoints or oceans apart—can now interact with one another with near immediacy and in high definition. While still miles away, anyone can be invited into another's space. We can welcome people into our businesses, into our classrooms and into our homes, no matter where they are located in the world. While the world may seem smaller, it certainly does not have to seem colder. These advances give us a chance to celebrate the best humanity has to offer.

Welcome

REFLECTION QUESTION

In what ways am I willing to be
more welcoming to others who are not where I am from?

WEEK 48

Welcome

I seek to welcome others into my space with the dignity of an ambassador and the warmth of family.

Day 2

CENTER

How does this week's reading CENTER me and bring calm, balance, and breathing space to my worldview?

Day 3

CALL

How does this week's reading CALL to me? How am I being awakened with a greater sense of purpose and spirituality? How am I inspired to be a force for good in the world?

Day 4

CHALLENGE

How does this week's reading CHALLENGE me to grow? What am I now ready to adjust, release, forgive, and accept as a result of this week's reading?

WEEK

48

Day 5 **CLARITY**

What new CLARITY have I gained as a result of this week's reading? What better understanding do I now possess?

Day 6 **COMFORT**

What brings me COMFORT about this week's reading? How am I more at ease or consoled by this week's reading?

Day 7 **CHANGE**

How am I CHANGED by this week's reading? What insights, transforming thoughts, inner realizations, overcomings and breakthroughs am I now experiencing?

"Life is not measured by the number of breaths you take but by the moments that take your breath away."
—Maya Angelou

I am one with all humankind.

"He drew a circle that shut me out—heretic, rebel, a thing to flout. But love and I had the wit to win: We drew a circle and took him in!"

— Edwin Markham

Xenophobia is fear, discrimination and hatred of other people simply because they are not from the same place where you are from. It is the erroneous habit among human beings to create inside and outside groups, drawing lines based upon differences. This habit of "otherizing" is dangerous because is feeds a false narrative about other humans and often leads to a dangerous social, political, and even spiritual environment for them in which to live.

When we are rooted in unconditional love, we become culturally curious and color brave. Understanding that love's true function is to unify, and harmonize all sentient life, we can trust that our explorations of language, food, art, dance, history, religion and the music of people from other countries will only serve to enhance our humanity and not diminish it.

REFLECTION QUESTION

In what ways can you open your mind and expand your heart to make room for all peoples of the Earth?

WEEK

49

I am one with all humankind.

Day 2 **CENTER**

How does this week's reading CENTER me and bring calm, balance, and breathing space to my worldview?

____

____

____

____

Day 3 **CALL**

How does this week's reading CALL to me? How am I being awakened with a greater sense of purpose and spirituality? How am I inspired to be a force for good in the world?

____

____

____

____

Day 4 **CHALLENGE**

How does this week's reading CHALLENGE me to grow? What am I now ready to adjust, release, forgive, and accept as a result of this week's reading?

____

____

____

____

WEEK

49

Day 5 **CLARITY**

What new CLARITY have I gained as a result of this week's reading? What better understanding do I now possess?

Day 6 **COMFORT**

What brings me COMFORT about this week's reading? How am I more at ease or consoled by this week's reading?

Day 7 **CHANGE**

How am I CHANGED by this week's reading? What insights, transforming thoughts, inner realizations, overcomings and breakthroughs am I now experiencing?

The more years I live, the more filled with life I become!

"Age is none of your spiritual business."
— Rev. Dr. Johnnie Colemon

"Sing them over again to me, wonderful words of life. Let me more of their beauty see, wonderful words of life." These are the lyrics of the hymn, "Wonderful Words of Life" written in 1874 by P.P. Bliss. And while these words were penned centuries ago, encoded in them is the fountain of youth. For words are living messengers and depending upon how we orchestrate them determines how much life force is released. Therefore, when we identify ourselves with age, rather than Life force, we align ourselves with the limitations associated with the number of years we have existed on the planet. As such, we form beliefs that set up mental and physical barriers that align with the number of days on the calendar since our physical birth.

Instead, as we begin to reclaim our spiritual identity, we can access the timeless, Eternal aspect of ourselves through affirming words of life. Life is a limitless, indestructible quality of Spirit that is forever vital, whole, energized, and perpetually self-renewing. Today, let us speak wonderful words of life and properly address and impress ourselves with the truth of our being and that is, we are eternally young.

REFLECTION QUESTION

In what ways may you be permitting your age to limit your Divine potential from being fully expressed?

The more years I live,
the more filled with life I become!.

Day 2 CENTER

How does this week's reading CENTER me and bring calm, balance, and breathing space to my worldview?

____

____

____

____

Day 3 CALL

How does this week's reading CALL to me? How am I being awakened with a greater sense of purpose and spirituality? How am I inspired to be a force for good in the world?

____

____

____

____

Day 4 CHALLENGE

How does this week's reading CHALLENGE me to grow? What am I now ready to adjust, release, forgive, and accept as a result of this week's reading?

____

____

____

____

WEEK

50

Day 5 **CLARITY**

What new CLARITY have I gained as a result of this week's reading? What better understanding do I now possess?

Day 6 **COMFORT**

What brings me COMFORT about this week's reading? How am I more at ease or consoled by this week's reading?

Day 7 **CHANGE**

How am I CHANGED by this week's reading? What insights, transforming thoughts, inner realizations, overcomings and breakthroughs am I now experiencing?

I AM a Miracle going somewhere to happen!

"I fairly sizzle with zeal and enthusiasm and spring forth with a mighty faith to do that which ought to be done by me."
— Charles Filmore

Zeal is the fire of the soul. Let it find you, fuel you, free you and feed you. It is lightning in a bottle, Omnipotence in concentrate, and energy on tap. It is the current that all big dreams surf upon. It is the bright red spontaneous splash of the artist's brush. It is the endless steam of the activist's march. It is the rushing adrenaline of the first responder. It is the unyielding persistence of the first-time laboring mother.

Zeal is a force like electricity and must be safely steered and lovingly leveraged. When it is overbalanced, we can burn up with revenge or burn out with exhaustion. When it is under balanced, we can shrivel up with depression or clam up with self-doubt. By connecting with that still small voice within, we become in tune with Divine timing that prompts us when to lower the flames of zeal to see clearly and when to raise the flames of zeal to act urgently.

REFLECTION QUESTION

What is burning in the fire
of your soul and where it is taking you?

WEEK 51

I AM a Miracle
going somewhere to happen!

Day 2

CENTER

How does this week's reading CENTER me and bring calm, balance, and breathing space to my worldview?

Day 3

CALL

How does this week's reading CALL to me? How am I being awakened with a greater sense of purpose and spirituality? How am I inspired to be a force for good in the world?

Day 4

CHALLENGE

How does this week's reading CHALLENGE me to grow? What am I now ready to adjust, release, forgive, and accept as a result of this week's reading?

WEEK

51

Day 5 CLARITY

What new CLARITY have I gained as a result of this week's reading? What better understanding do I now possess?

Day 6 COMFORT

What brings me COMFORT about this week's reading? How am I more at ease or consoled by this week's reading?

Day 7 CHANGE

How am I CHANGED by this week's reading? What insights, transforming thoughts, inner realizations, overcomings and breakthroughs am I now experiencing?

My zest for living draws unto me opportunities to experience life in colorful, flavorful and dynamic ways.

"What hunger is in relation to food, zest is in relation to life."

— Bertrand Russell

Cooking carries with it the perfect metaphor for life. We visit our favorite restaurants anticipating a satisfying and filling meal. The preparation, the presentation, and the atmosphere are as important to the experience as the food itself. Yet the most important aspect of the experience is the flavor we often add in an effort to give the food that zip, zing or pop. A sprinkle of salt, a dash of pepper, a pat of butter, or a dip in the sauce provides that final element of flavor, color and zest, which heightens the experience.

Our experiences in life, at its best, like food, can be nourishing and filling for sure, but may require that we add a "certain something" of ourselves to the mix. The hunger and passion we bring to the table can add to the exhilaration of the experience. Zest exhibited in the forms of anticipation, attentiveness, glee and delight can turn even the dull and distasteful into something flavorful and memorable.

REFLECTION QUESTION

What flavors of character
can you add to make someone's life better?

WEEK
52

My zest for living draws unto me opportunities to experience life in colorful, flavorful and dynamic ways.

Day 2

CENTER

How does this week's reading CENTER me and bring calm, balance, and breathing space to my worldview?

____

____

____

____

Day 3

CALL

How does this week's reading CALL to me? How am I being awakened with a greater sense of purpose and spirituality? How am I inspired to be a force for good in the world?

____

____

____

____

Day 4

CHALLENGE

How does this week's reading CHALLENGE me to grow? What am I now ready to adjust, release, forgive, and accept as a result of this week's reading?

____

____

____

____

WEEK

52

Day 5 **CLARITY**

What new CLARITY have I gained as a result of this week's reading? What better understanding do I now possess?

Day 6 **COMFORT**

What brings me COMFORT about this week's reading? How am I more at ease or consoled by this week's reading?

Day 7 **CHANGE**

How am I CHANGED by this week's reading? What insights, transforming thoughts, inner realizations, overcomings and breakthroughs am I now experiencing?

Special Acknowledgments

(Kevin Kitrell Ross)

There are four people who constantly top the list that are the interlocking unit that is always there inspiring me to savor more of life's beauty, to tiptoe through the tulips and to enjoy the breeze. Anita, Angelina, Kameela, and Khaiden, thank you for being my Breathing Space, my shelter, my inspiration, and my peace. Every line and space in these pages form the music my heart sings for you and the freedom I dream for you all to enjoy, in the world we are each endeavoring to build — one breath at a time.

To my "Brother Rev" Eric Ovid Donaldson, thank you for your deep yes in taking this journey in service with me. Thank you for your implicit agreement for over 30 years to touching lives, ceasing injustice, launching dreamers, jumping to the frontlines of fairness and anchoring heaven. Thank you for coming alongside me to clear the barriers, set the foundation, and build the bridge to Beloved Community.

To Rhonda Gutierrez, renowned visual artist and photographer and our life-long friend, thank you for saying with your beautiful images what we have attempted to say with words. You nailed it!

To my amazing colleague and publisher, Renita Bryant and her phenomenal creative and editorial team at Mynd Matters Publishing, a deep bow of gratitude to you for your unmatched professionalism, clarity and for holding me accountable to bringing my dreams for the world into reality. You are my very own "sister mogul" and it is my joy to take this journey with you and your team.

To the spiritual community and Board of Trustees at Unity of Sacramento International Spiritual Center, you are oxygen for all that I have been purposed to do. It has been my joy to know you, love you, serve you, and grow with you for over a decade. Thank you for being the hub where diverse worlds merge and a glimpse of the greater good is found and celebrated.

I would also wish to acknowledge my amazing Dream Team, whose leadership, hard work, tireless dedication, humor, unwavering commitment to the vision and boundless energy and creativity push me to dream a bigger dream. To my brother Rev. Charlie Cooper, Jr., Rev. Eric Donaldson, Mrs. Suhir Bruce, Ms. Ajani Reign Thompson, Ms. Janelle Smalls, Mr. Chris Kigar, Ms. Yehansu Teldsa, and Farrah Lester, thank you for weathering the most unparalleled time in known American history, with a spirit of resilience, grace and zeal! I love you all and I would choose you all over again.

To national team of freedom fighters and fellow light warriors, Ryan McClinton, Pastor Les Simmons, Ebony Harper, Dereca Blackmon, Rev. Julie Moret, Dr. David Alexander, Melissa Hull, Bishop Jack Bomar, Gabby Trejo, Basim Elkarra, Katie Loncke, Rev. Charles Taylor, and Rev. Charline Manual, let's stay the course. Next stop, over the top! The Leadership Council of the Association for Global New Thought, Board of Sacramento Area Congregations Together, my Colleagues in the American Leadership Forum and the 12.

Finally, to all the countless families of our untimely ancestors created by race-based violence, continue to breathe! "The Gladiators of Justice are riding, the coming of their cadence can be heard. The moment of truth is arising and Love will have the final word."

Special Acknowledgments
(Eric Ovid Donaldson)

We wish to acknowledge all those who attend and appreciate our Breathing Space services at Unity of Sacramento, and all who appreciate the practice of meditation, reflection and journaling.

To my spiritual brother and colleague Rev. Kevin Kitrell Ross, who finally convinced me to make the move to California so we could work together more readily and more often. To do this work with my best friend of 30 years (and still be friends) is outstanding.

Thank you Unity of Sacramento Meditation Leaders Dr. Kristee Haggins, Marybeth Moore, David Cook, and Brenda Davis who year in and year out prepared themselves to sit in the purple meditation chair each Sunday.

To my childhood friends, Thomas Calhoun, Fred Williamson, Alan Stewart, Daniel Tucker and Jeffrey West, who all saw something special in me from the start, and decided to remain my friends anyway. Thanks for letting me be me.

To my friend Rev. Robert JV McMillan, a wonderful photographer who captured magical moments of me and my family over the years with his special gift. Because of you I have documented memories I get to keep and share with others (especially one particular memory in this book).

My son and daughter, Davon and Deja Donaldson, who allow their father the time away to complete this project.

My parents, Ruby and Etheridge Donaldson, who forged for me an amazing spiritual foundation and legacy.

Thank you to my brothers and sister Etheredge, Duane (transitioned) and Angela Donaldson who keep me grounded.

An eternal bow to my spiritual mentors, who are now ancestors; Rev. David Williamson, Rev. Johnnie Colemon, Rev. Frederick Eikerenkoetter, Father George Clements, Rev. Ann Jefferson, Rev. Mary Tumpkin and Rev. Ruth Mosley.

To my spiritual family at Unity Christian Church of Memphis, where I pastored for nearly seven years. Thank you for the magnificent memories and the wonderful work we did in the world together.

To Rev. Lameteria Hall for her sister-like support during difficult times.

David Nolley and Van Johnson, Carol Pitts for simply believing in me.

And a very special acknowledgement to my wife, the late Rev. Valencia Dillon-Donaldson, whose commitment with women and children in recovery, and 18 years of marriage continues to inspire and strengthen me.

About the Authors

For over twenty five years, Kevin Kitrell Ross has been on a mission to inspire people to awaken to their highest potential and be a force for good in the world. This mission has taken him around the world serving people as an internationally renowned keynote speaker, panelist, author, radio talk show host, master life coach and most prominently, as the Senior Minister of Unity of Sacramento International Spiritual Center.

"Rev. Kev," as he is affectionately called, is also deeply committed to co-creating a world of peace, prosperity and unconditional love for all and has risen as a respected interfaith social justice leader. Ross has earned a reputation as a bridge-builder and has worked nationally and internationally to heal the widening global racial and religious gap. He has shared the stage with luminaries ranging from His Holiness, the Dalai Lama, President Nelson Mandela to Vice President Kamala Harris, to Dr. Marian Wright Edelman.

He serves on the Leadership Council of the Association for Global New Thought, a Senior Fellow of the Mountain-Valley Chapter of the American Leadership Forum, and a Board member of Sacramento Area Congregations Together.

Ross is a popular interview guest for numerous magazines, newspapers, blogs, radio and national television shows - making a recent appearance with Oprah on an Oprah Winfrey Network special. He is a graduate of Morehouse College, a three-time humanitarian award recipient, and an inductee into the Martin Luther King, Jr. International Clergy Hall of Honor.

He considers among his highest honors being invited to pray for the nation, when he opened a session of the United States House of Representatives. Rev. Kev. is married to Anita Ross, founder of the Women for Equality movement, and together they have three children.

With over thirty years of leadership experience, Eric Ovid Donaldson's mission is simple—he is dedicated to the discovery, development and perfect unfoldment of the divine potential inherent in all humanity.

"Rev. E," as he is affectionately called, is the Senior Associate Minister of Operations at Unity of Sacramento, and is also an instructor at the Unity Urban Ministerial School (an affiliate of Unity Worldwide Ministries).

Among his many accomplishments, Rev. E placed first in his Semi-Final Round of the 2014 Toastmasters International World Championship of Public Speaking. He is also a member of the Board of Preachers at the prestigious Martin Luther King, Jr. International Chapel at Morehouse College. His work as a healer, and with people from all walks of life has resulted in numerous awards and acknowledgements including a day named in his honor in the city of Memphis, Tennessee.

Rev. E enjoyed nearly eighteen years of marriage to his late wife Valencia and together they have raised two beautiful teenagers.

CPSIA information can be obtained
at www.ICGtesting.com
Printed in the USA
BVHW041703030221
599297BV00013B/101

9 781953 307378